NINETEENTH-CENTURY
FASHION
IN DETAIL

NINETEENTH-CENTURY FASHION IN DETAIL

Lucy Johnston

with Marion Kite and Helen Persson

Photographs by Richard Davis
Drawings by Leonie Davis

V&A Publications

I would like to thank the following people: Richard Davis for his superb photography; Lara Flecker, whose excellent mounting skills shine through in the full-length shots; Rita Brown, who brought so many of the garments to life with her wonderful mounting; Leonie Davis for her meticulous line drawings; Helen Persson and Marion Kite for their fascinating text, including entries on straw-work, fur, feathers and flowers (initials mark contributions); Rhona Ferling, Lara Rayburn and Jennifer Nicholason for their help in preparing objects for photography.

I am also grateful to other colleagues at the V&A, including Christopher Wilk, Linda Parry, Susan North, Clare Browne, Jennifer Wearden, Frances Collard, Charlotte Samuels, Suzanne Smith, Jenny Lister, Lynda Hillyer, Albertina Cogram, Frances Hartog, Elizabeth-Anne Haldane, Mary Butler, Monica Woods, Frances Ambler, Ken Jackson, Christopher Breward, Rosemary Crill, Boris Pretzel and Joanna Whalley.

I would also like to thank Avril Hart; Peter FitzGerald, Elizabeth Dineley and Christopher Bryant; Annabel Westman; Philip Parker and Keith Levett, Henry Poole & Co.; Hugh Cheape and Fiona Anderson, National Museums of Scotland; Rosemary Harden, The Museum of Costume, Bath; Gillian Brewer, National Army Museum; Françoise Tétart-Vittu, Anna Zazzo, Rebecca Leger and Corinne Dom, Musée Galliera, Musée de la Mode de la Ville de Paris; Jean-Paul Leclercq, Musée de la Mode et du Textile, Paris; Dr Celia Fisher, Royal Botanic Gardens, Kew; the book's designer Cara Gallardo and editor Rachel Connolly; and Malcolm Johnston for his enduring support.

Funding for the line drawings included in this book was generously provided by Claudine Malone.

First published by V&A Publications, 2005

V&A Publications
160 Brompton Road
London SW3 1HW

ISBN 978 1 851 77439 5

10 9 8 7 6 5 4
2011 2010 2009 2008

A catalogue record for this book is available from the British Library.

Designed by Area
Conservation: Lara Flecker, Albertina Cogram, Frances Hartog, Elizabeth-Anne Haldane, Marion Kite
Costume consultant: Rita Brown
Photographs by Richard Davis, V&A Photographic Studio
Drawings by Leonie Davis

Front cover illustration: Cerise taffeta bodice, skirt and peplum, 1869–70 (back view, detail). T.118-1979, see p.126.

Back cover illustrations (all details), clockwise from top left: Man's nightgown, 1815–22. Circ.718-1912, see p.116; red cotton and brown leather corset, 1880s. T.84-1980, see p.144; bodice with purple pleated silk chiffon insert, 1880–90. T.206-1927, see p.174; velvet bodice embroidered with birds, 1870s. T.871-1913, see p.208.

Frontispiece: Pink satin corset, 1890s. T.378-1974, see p.118.

Printed in Singapore by C. S. Graphics

V&A Publications
160 Brompton Road
London SW3 1HW
www.vam.ac.uk

CONTENTS

INTRODUCTION

Many of the influences, innovations and stylistic changes that shaped nineteenth-century fashion are brought to life by the garments illustrated in this book. The delicate embroidery on neo-classical gowns, elegant tailoring on men's coats, vibrant colours of artificial dyes and profusion of ornate trimmings reveal some of the details which make this period so rich. They also show how a woman's silhouette was transformed during this era through whalebone corsets, cage crinolines, bustles and skilful garment construction.

Most of the clothes illustrated belonged to middle and upper class men and women and were at the height of fashion for their time. Many were worn during the day, others for sumptuous evening occasions, and some for popular sports such as riding and cycling. As well as conforming to fashionable styles, they often reveal the personal tastes of the wearer. A vest worn by the Fifth Marquis of Anglesey, for example, was made by one of the best shirtmakers in Paris, but also displays his flamboyant personality in choice of colour and an embroidered coronet (page 32). Some of the clothes have also been altered or remade to adapt them to the latest fashions, for special occasions, changes to the figure, or because they were originally worn by someone else.

While it covers many of the details and intricacies of dress, this book is not a comprehensive study of nineteenth-century fashion. It focuses on objects in the V&A's collection, many of which have survived for aesthetic, historical or sentimental reasons, as accidents of fate and, most significantly, through the care of the donors. Fashionable women's dress, for example, tended to be preserved because of its attractive colour, design and materials. It is therefore represented in larger numbers than men's garments, which by the beginning of the nineteenth century had become much plainer, decorative appeal being replaced by the subtleties of cut and construction. The changes in men's fashion were also less conspicuous than women's, so coats could be worn until they were threadbare or were passed on second hand. British styles also predominate, although many of the clothes show fashionable influences from abroad, including a man's cloak embroidered in Kashmir for the European market (page 102) and a bodice made in Paris by Worth (page 64). The text therefore reflects the garments that survive and concentrates on British upper and middle class fashions.

The book is arranged along thematic lines, covering subjects ranging from technological innovations to the passion for historical revival in fashion, which illustrate some of the major themes running through nineteenth-century dress. These themes are designed to provide an entry point through which the reader can study individual objects in greater depth. Because articles of clothing can tell so many different stories and reflect a variety of influences, subjects other than those relating to the main chapter theme may be covered in the individual entries. These include etiquette, construction, stylistic change, fabric design, and information about when and where the garment was worn as well as who it belonged to.

Within the chapters, costume is also grouped together to illustrate a particular aspect of its theme. The first five garments in *The Male Image*, for example, explore the way fashion borrowed and reinterpreted trimmings from military dress, particularly during the period of the Napoleonic Wars. In *Construction Details*, pages 156 to 164 describe tailoring methods and how they were applied to men's and women's clothing. These sections are not visibly divided but should become apparent when reading the text and studying the photographs and line drawings.

The Male Image examines men's dress as well as its influence on women's sportswear and tailored styles. It reveals how military trimmings were adapted for civilian use, as seen in the decoration on a woman's riding habit (page 16) and walking dress (page 20), which is reminiscent of the parallel lines of braiding extending across the breast of many uniforms. The increase in tailored styles for women is also explored, showing how, by the late nineteenth century, the masculine-style coat had been adopted for many outdoor activities. Many of these garments were given existing masculine names such as 'frock coats', 'Ulsters', 'Chesterfields', 'Newmarket' and 'Eton' jackets. A jaunty seaside dress on page 28 illustrates the influence of the sailor suit on fashion, popularized for fashionable wear by the Prince of Wales (Edward VII, 1841–1910). Examples of men's morning coats show typical masculine styles of the 1870s with their wide lapels and slanting foreparts. Finally, a range of men's sporting attire reflects the popularity of hunting, shooting and archery, as well as the impact of new pastimes, such as cycling, on dress.

Historicism explores the different ways in which styles from previous centuries were revived and reinterpreted in fashionable dress. Delicate muslin dresses evoke neo-classical designs inspired by Greek and Roman statuary, while 'puffed' and 'slashed' trimmings are reminiscent of decoration on Tudor dress. Two dresses on pages 50 and 52 are made from 1770s silks and show how the delicate colours and patterns complemented contemporary tastes. The eighteenth century also provided inspiration for late nineteenth-century fashions, including the creations of Charles Frederick Worth. Another important influence was the tartan frenzy fuelled by a keen antiquarian interest in Highland dress during the early nineteenth century. A waistcoat and woman's cloak show how most of the patterns worn in the nineteenth century were fairly recent inventions, despite claims of their being rooted in clan tradition dating back hundreds of years (page 70).

Romantic Styles looks at garments that are charming, pretty, or that capture a sense of romantic fantasy. Delicate gauze gowns reveal the soft, dreamy look that characterized much fashionable 1820s evening wear, evocative colours such as 'maiden's-blush rose' adding to their ethereal quality. The enormous sleeves, tiny waists and fluttering ribbons on 1830s dresses epitomize historical romantic exuberance, especially when given names such as 'Cavalier', 'Medici' and 'Donna Maria'. Men's clothing did not escape these influences, and frock coats with cape-like collars, nipped-in waists and full skirts reflected details of women's costume. An American wedding dress of shimmering silk satin shows how prosperous brides often wore white and later adapted their gowns for romantic evening wear (page 86). Towards the end of the century trends were moving towards a soft, dreamy, light look, a style embodied in an opera cloak by Jean-Philippe Worth, where a froth of lace and fine silk chiffon cascades from the neck and shoulders (page 88). Huge puffed sleeves swelling out of an 1895 day dress illustrate how sleeves similar to the romantic creations of the 1830s were returning to the height of fashion (page 90).

Exoticism shows how other cultures influenced Western fashion, aided by the trappings of trade and Empire. Designs on shoes, gowns and outdoor garments reveal how fabrics were woven or embroidered in India and the Middle East for the European market. They often present hybrid patterns largely dictated by Western tastes. Other textiles were based on Indian patterns but printed in Britain. Exotic animals were used to make and trim fashionable clothes and accessories such as the hummingbird and beetle fan (page 108) and the man's slipper covered in the skin of the golden or olive sea snake (page 106). Dress was also styled to look out of the ordinary, although the materials used were commonplace. An eye-catching cape, for example, appears exotic but is largely made of feathers from domestic fowl (page 114), while a man's flannel nightgown is decorated with wool tufts simulating ermine to give it a luxurious appearance (page 116).

Innovations explores how the development of new technologies affected dress and the way it was made. Striking gowns reverberating with colour illustrate how natural and synthetic dyes were used to generate the dazzling hues that became particularly fashionable in Britain during the 1850s and 1860s. Crinoline cages and the style of garments worn over them show how these flexible spring-steel structures distended the skirts, liberating women from layers of heavy petticoats. Improvements in design, equipment and materials helped corsets mould the female figure to the slimmer silhouette which marked fashion from the 1870s onwards. The sewing machine also had a huge impact on the construction and manufacture of clothing, and two dresses of the mid-1880s demonstrate how it saved time but also encouraged the use of complex decoration (page 148). Less noticeable but important innovations were also evident in men's dress, such as the introduction of new fastening devices on the back of waistcoats and improvements to the design of braces. The chapter also discusses improved construction methods in men's tailoring, the development of machine-made bobbin net, new styles and shapes such as bustles, and why red was adopted in the early nineteenth century for hunting dress.

Construction Details exemplifies some of the methods of making which particularly define nineteenth-century dress. British tailors were renowned for their skill in manipulating cloth, and a variety of methods and measuring systems were promoted to improve coat-cutting. Details and line drawings of coats, pockets and linings reveal how cutting and construction techniques helped shape the garment to suit the individual as well as his or her personal tastes. Some dressmakers also showed great attention to detail, as illustrated in the two beautifully finished bodice linings on page 168 with their notched and carefully pressed seam allowances and whalebone strips inserted into immaculately finished casings. Many nineteenth-century garments were pleated and gathered to reduce fullness and also to provide decoration, and the dresses on pages 172 and 174 demonstrate some of the ways this was achieved. As seen throughout the book, a wealth of trimmings, including lace, satin, feathers and fur, were applied to women's garments of all descriptions. The final section of this chapter focuses on passementerie, such as tassels, cord, fringe and pompoms, which adorned many dresses and mantles.

The Natural World explores the fascination for plant life and the extensive use of fur and feathers which resulted in massive imports of dead birds and animal skins. Fabrics printed and woven with floral and foliate designs as well as fine embroidery show how this was a popular form of decoration on men's and women's dress throughout the century. Inspiration came from a variety of sources, including botanical engravings, pattern books and plants grown in gardens or conservatories, and some dresses were even designed to imitate trees. Many of the plants illustrated are recognizable and include nasturtiums, anemones, vine-leaves, irises, heather and roses, although a lot of the colours are not true to life. Realistic depictions of fruit also appear on dress fabrics, and the strawberries and oranges on pages 192 and 202 look good enough to eat! Insects were another source of inspiration, and straw-work bees, chenille ladybirds and embroidered moths adorn garments of the 1860s and 1870s; sometimes they were so realistic that they were mistaken for the real thing. Unfortunately the bird perched on a woman's hat of the 1880s (page 212) is genuine, as are the skins of thirty-two wolves used to line a gentleman's fur coat (page 216) and the numerous mink tails which trim the mantle on page 218.

The garments illustrated in these chapters spring from the page with a beauty and freshness that often belies their age and fragility. Rich colours, luxurious trimmings, skilful construction, changing silhouettes and choice of fabric provide a valuable insight into many aspects of nineteenth-century fashion and production techniques. The past can inform the present, and these elegant clothes will surely capture the imagination and inspire designers, students, researchers, collectors and lovers of fashion well into the future.

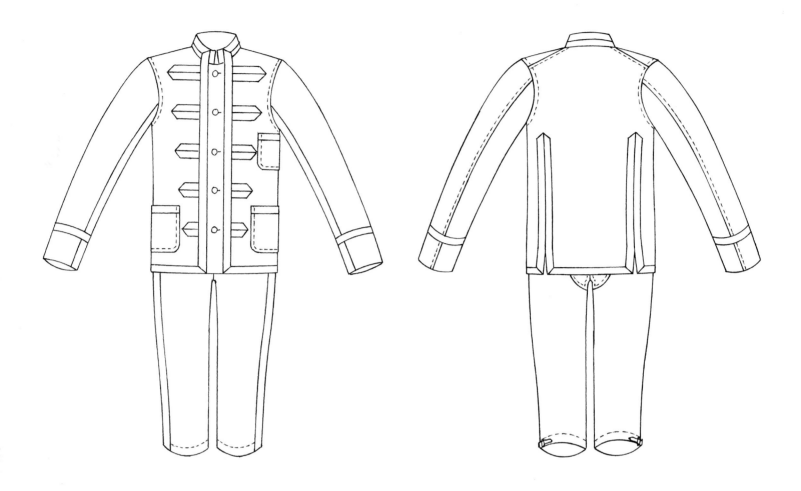

This American jacket forms part of a cycling club uniform. The late 1870s saw a revival of bicycling in the United States due to the advent of the 'high-wheeler', better known as the penny-farthing. These large machines could be dangerous and awkward to handle, so many novices joined cycling clubs for advice and instruction. A uniform gave members a sense of belonging and also an appropriate costume for the perils of the road. Colours varied from club to club but grey was popular as it helped disguise dirt and bicycle oil. Experts also recommended that every garment be made of wool which, unlike cotton or linen, supposedly prevented chills.

This jacket is made of machine-knitted jersey, which is lightweight, relatively quick drying and more supple than tweed. It is constructed in the style of a military patrol jacket[1], a design favoured by many clubs. The mandarin collar and silk-covered buttons fastening right up to the throat give the jacket a degree of neatness and formality. Rows of braiding down the foreparts and across the breast have a practical as well as decorative appeal. G. Lacy Hillier, a member of the British Cyclists' Touring Club, stated that 'flat bars of braid sewn ... across the chest of a military or cycling uniform, are remarkably efficacious in preventing the jacket from stretching, and losing its shape'.[2] The matching breeches have a double-seat constructed from two semi-circular panels of knitted fabric which are seamed together and reinforced with a cotton lining. Although popular at first, many cyclists found double-seats uncomfortable as the thickness of the fabric rucked on the saddle, and the seams sometimes caused blisters.

By the mid-1890s uniforms and braiding were going out of fashion, largely due to the widespread introduction of the safety bicycle and air-filled tyres. Such developments made cycling accessible to growing numbers of men and women and lessened the need to belong to a club or adopt a specific uniform.

1. The patrol jacket had many regimental variations in trimmings, including braid, fur and astrakhan.
2. G. Lacy Hillier and Viscount Bury, *Cycling* (London, 1887), p.230.

Man's cycling suit: patrol jacket and knee-breeches.
Made of machine-knitted jersey fastened with silk-covered buttons and trimmed with mohair braid.
Marshall E. Smith & Bro., Philadelphia. USA, 1887–90
T.7-2000

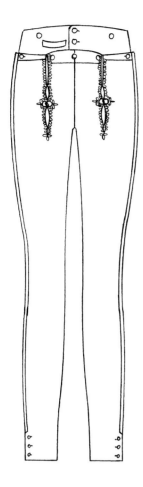 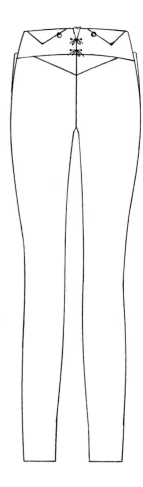

An intricate pattern of loops and applied braid decorates the front of this pair of men's pantaloons. Pantaloons were a form of close-fitting trousers or tights introduced into fashionable dress during the 1790s. They complemented the close-fitting lines of early nineteenth-century men's coats as they were shaped to the leg, often ending just above the ankle where button fastenings or straps kept them in place. Although difficult to cut and put together without causing unsightly creases or wrinkles when the leg was moved, they could look extremely elegant. The tailor J. Golding extolled their merits in his publication of 1818: 'This is an article of dress very generally worn, and when made to fit well, are [sic] exceedingly neat and convenient, as they may be worn either with gaiters, boots, or over stockings only.'[1]

Pantaloons also brought the glamour of military uniform into men's fashionable dress, especially when teamed with Hessian boots.[2] Uniforms worn by the various armies during the Napoleonic Wars (1793–1815) were often very colourful and lavishly adorned with braid and tassels. It is hardly surprising that some of these attractive trimmings should have infiltrated fashion, particularly when nationalistic feelings ran high. Civilian pantaloons were often ornamented with military-style braid that was applied in a vertical band of topside Russia braiding. They were not, however, generally decorated on the front, which suggests that this pair was for military use. The silk braid is applied in the form of an Austrian knot, which was a popular motif on pantaloons of the light cavalry such as the hussars and light dragoons.

1. J. Golding, *Golding's Tailor's Assistant* (London, 1817–18), p.43.

2. The Hessian boot reached to just below the knee and was cut with a peak at the front decorated by a tassel. It was originally associated with the light cavalry.

Man's pantaloons made of machine-knitted cotton decorated with applied silk braid.
British, 1810–20
Given by Lady Osborn
T.41-1986

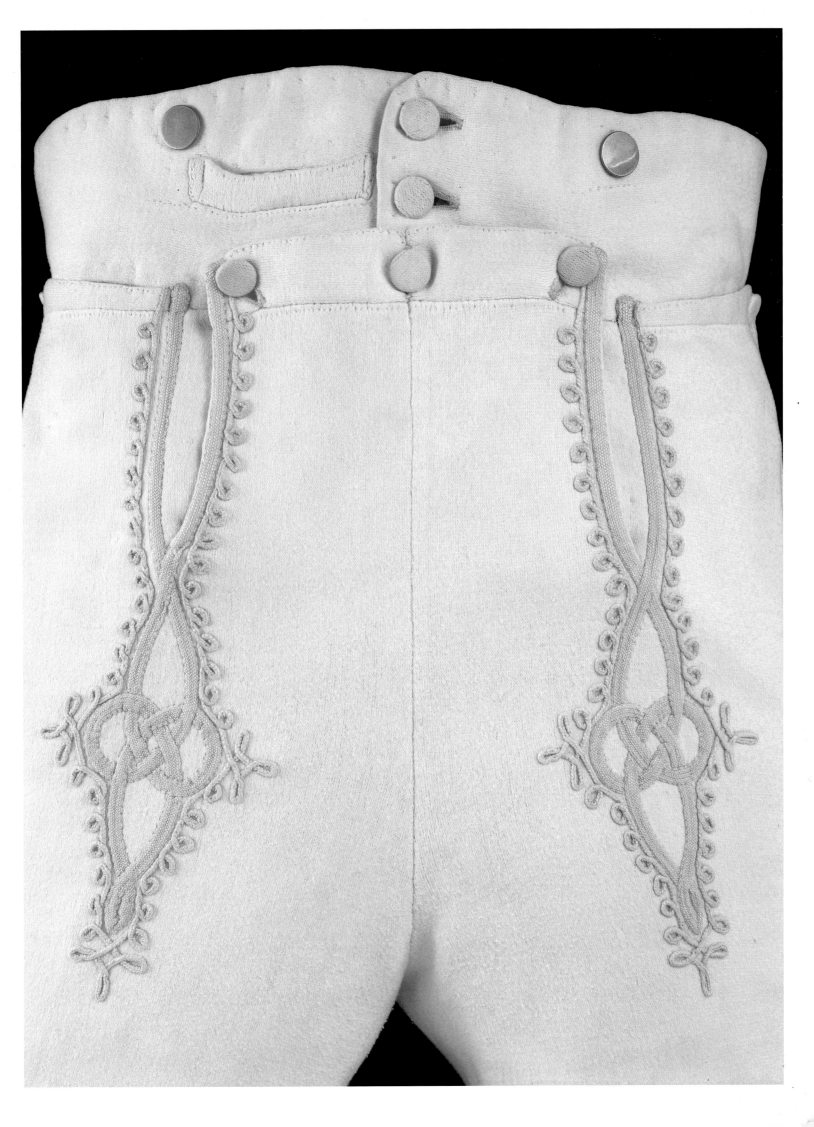

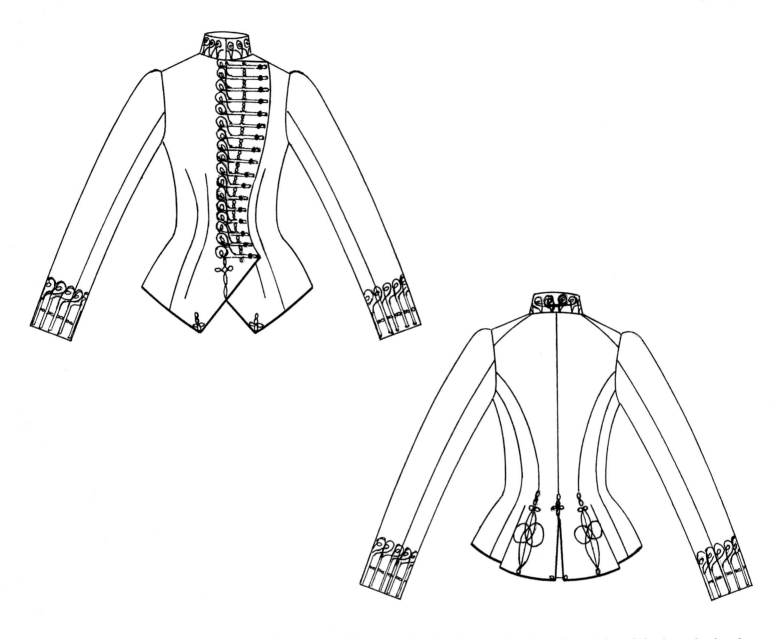

Masculine styles had long been a feature of the female riding habit. For much of the nineteenth century fashionable women wore dark woollen tailored jackets inspired by men's coats. By the 1880s their dress was so similar that some observers noted that from a distance it was difficult to distinguish very young ladies from young gentlemen. This was no doubt helped by the fashion for wearing bowlers, top hats, cravats, waistcoats and trousers under skirts.

Many women's jackets were embellished with details borrowed from military uniform. Braiding was a popular form of decoration inspired by ornamentation on regimental dress as well as the flamboyant hussar designs.[1] This elegant example is based on the regimental patrol jacket characterized by parallel rows of applied braid across the breast, looped at intervals into designs known as 'crow's feet' because of their distinctive shape. Here the rows are shortened, and fanciful whirls at the proper right edge and on the collar do not relate to military models. This imaginative combination of vertical and horizontal trimming emphasizes the length of the bodice rather than its width and ensures that the waist appears relatively small.

The tailoring firm Redfern and Co. made this riding jacket for May Primrose Littledale. They were famous for their sporting costumes, smart tailor-made dresses and coats suited to everyday fashionable wear. During the mid-1880s Redfern incorporated braiding into many of their designs for walking outfits and outdoor jackets. *The Queen* magazine of 10 May 1884 commented on some particularly striking examples including, 'The "Hungarian" … lavishly adorned with finest mohair braid, and finished with knotted cords; and the "Polish", of royal blue "faced" cloth … handsomely braided across the front.' Unfortunately May did not have long to enjoy wearing this jacket as she died in a riding accident shortly after it was made.

1. The hussars were light cavalry regiments and their uniform was particularly decorative as it was derived from Hungarian national dress.

Woman's riding jacket of flannel trimmed with mohair and lined with sateen. Fastened with hooks and eyes beneath the ornamental loop and button fastening.
Messrs Redfern and Co. English, 1885–86
Given by the Honourable Mrs S. F. Tyser
T.430-1990

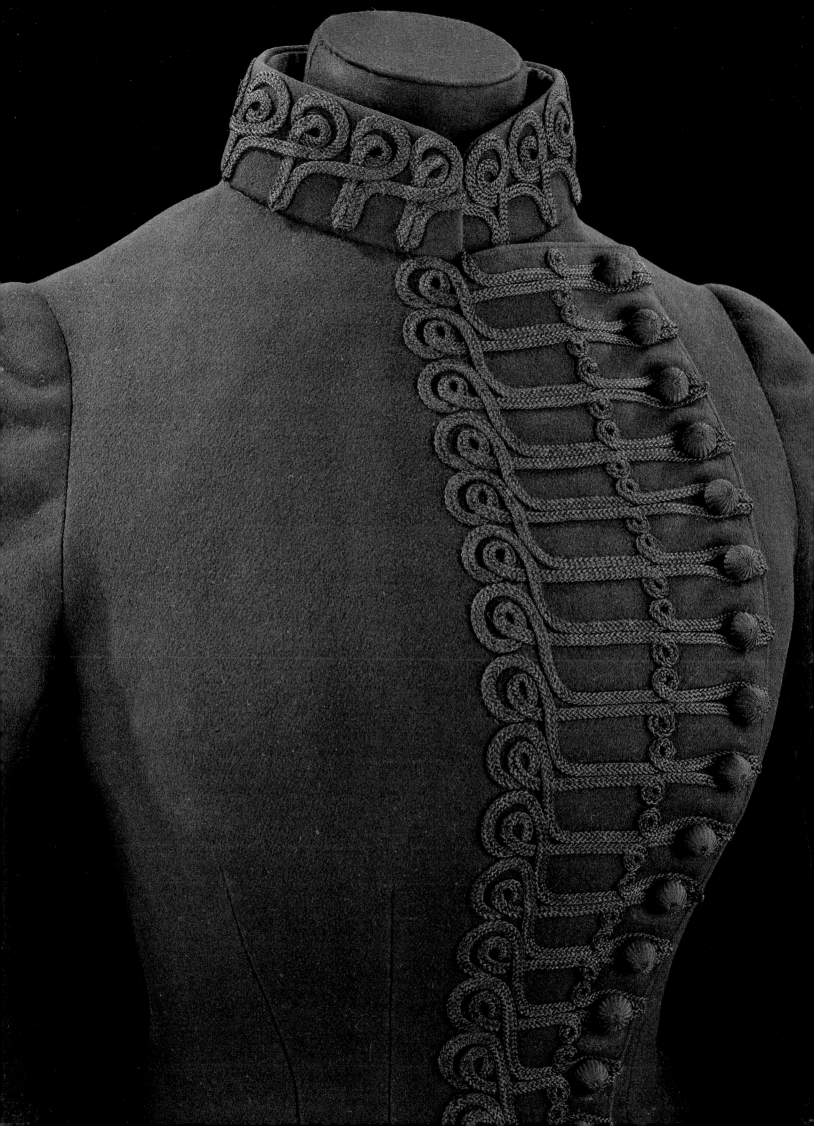

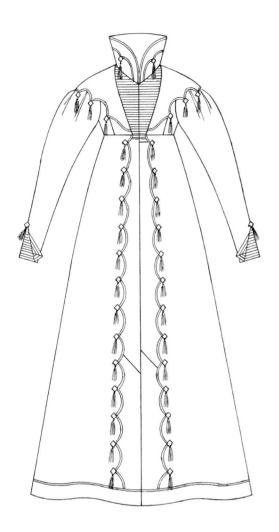
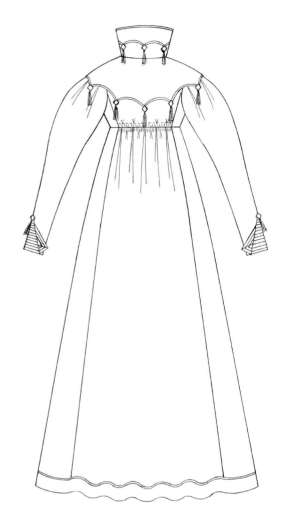

Decorative trimmings and imaginative construction enhance many early nineteenth-century women's sleeves. Here, applied panels of pleated silk give the impression that the cuff is turned back to reveal a layer of fabric underneath. It is actually the patterned silk that has been slit vertically at the wrist and folded to provide a backing fabric for the triangular wings. The diagonal and vertical pleats create an interesting visual effect and a perfectly placed tassel anchors the design. Pleated silk decorates the front of the pelisse to match the sleeves.

The pointed shape of the cuff is reminiscent of cuffs on British light cavalry uniforms dating back to the late eighteenth century. It became very fashionable to borrow regimental trimmings, and an outdoor garment provided an ideal vehicle for display. The bodice also follows military models as it resembles the plastron fronts on regimental dress, derived from lancers' jackets. The word plastron comes from the Italian for breastplate, and in military terms was originally a panel of fabric placed across the chest and attached by two rows of vertical buttons. The high stand collar is equally military in style, although, like the rest of the garment, light, delicate materials give it a feminine appeal.

Woman's pelisse of silk decorated with applied panels of pleated silk and trimmed with tassels. Lined with silk.
British, about 1820
Given by Miss Marion Dawson
T.357-1920

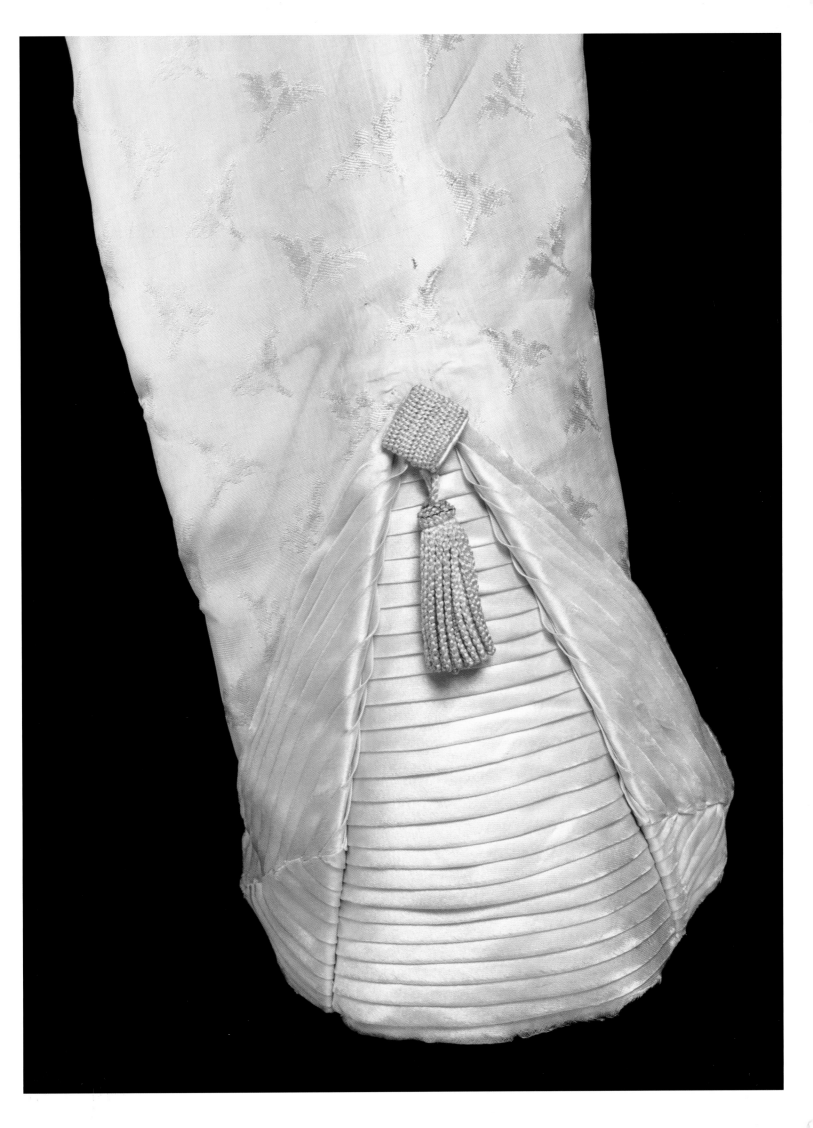

Echoes of military uniform give this walking dress a masculine flourish. The curving satin bands applied to the front of the spencer are reminiscent of the parallel lines of braiding which extended across the breast of many uniforms. Passementerie in the form of crescent-shaped moulds[1], looped cord and balls covered in floss silk replace the gilt or silver buttons on some regimental coats. The tassels on the collar ends and cuff bands evoke the tassels adorning boots, hats, sashes and cap lines of military accessories. In place of epaulettes, puffed oversleeves composed of linked bows emphasize the shoulder line.

This infusion of military styles into fashionable dress was largely due to the influence of the Napoleonic Wars (1793–1815). Among other factors, contact with foreign troops had a strong impact on civilian as well as regimental dress, and military ornament was translated into stylish trimmings on women's hats, bodices, spencers and pelisses. The uniforms worn during this period were some of the most elaborate in the history of military dress, and their bright colours, frogging, braid and tassels fuelled the imagination of fashion for years to come.

Although this walking outfit is not based on any particular uniform, some garments closely followed certain styles. The uniform of the hussars, who were light cavalry, was particularly flamboyant as it was derived from Hungarian national dress. In her memoirs, Elizabeth Grant describes the admiration she received when she 'walked out like a hussar in a dark cloth pelisse trimmed with fur and braided like the coat of a staff-officer, boots to match, and a fur cap set on one side, and kept on the head by means of a cord with long tassels'.[2]

1. Moulds were traditionally made of turned wood and came in a variety of forms, including steeple, mosque, onion and boule.

2. Elizabeth Grant, *Memoirs of a Highland Lady 1797–1827* (Edinburgh, 1988), Vol. 2, p.10.

Walking dress (spencer, skirt and bodice) of silk with applied silk satin panels. Trimmed with passementerie.
British, 1817–20
Given by Mrs A. Wallinger
T.110-1969

During the 1880s and 1890s, jackets and coats based on masculine styles became a popular feature in the woman's wardrobe. Frock coats, Ulsters, Chesterfields, Newmarket and Eton jackets appeared on the pages of fashion magazines, metamorphosed into close-fitting and narrow-waisted ladies' garments. The glimpse of a crisp white shirt collar and cravat underneath added the finishing touch to this manly look. This style was so admired that one tailoring manual reported: 'A lady despises, so far as tailor-made garments are concerned, any name or designation which borders on the feminine. The more like men's garments in appearance they are made, the more manlike the names we give their garments, the better they like it.'[1]

The jacket in this image was known as the double-breasted Reefer and was based on the loose-fitting man's garment of the same name. It was very popular for spring wear when women cast off their heavy overcoats in preference for warm jackets. Distinguishing features included wide lapels with double or even triple-stitched edges, up to six large buttons (three on each side) and flapped pockets on the hips. Discreet feminine flourishes were permitted, such as the leaf-shaped revers, glossy braid snaking down the foreparts and the full sleeves pinched into darts at the top.

1. T.H. Holding, *Late Victorian Women's Tailoring* (London, 1897), p.35.

Woman's double-breasted Reefer made of boxcloth trimmed with applied silk Russia braid.
British, 1892–97
Given by Mrs Pickthorn
T.70-1954

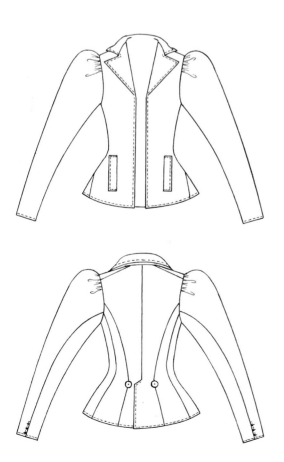

As women engaged in a wider range of activities more practical clothing styles were adopted. Tailor-made outfits such as this one helped meet the needs of a diverse lifestyle. Plain woollen costumes were considered ideal for a variety of leisure pursuits and could be adapted for sports such as shooting and golf. They may not have been more comfortable than other styles, but the hard-wearing fabric and relative lack of trimmings made them easier to care for and very versatile.

Style was not necessarily sacrificed for function, as elegant, close-fitting designs graced the pages of tailoring journals. Some featured jackets and skirts in contrasting checks, stripes and diagonals; others, like this one, were made of the same material throughout. Vests based on the man's waistcoat were another popular feature. Here the jacket is semi-fitted with no shaping in the front or fastenings so that it shows off the waistcoat underneath. The pearly tones of the buttons complement the soft colour of the cloth, and the ruffled frill on the stand collar adds a delicate touch.

Woman's tailored jacket ensemble made of tweed lined with silk twill and fastened with mother-of-pearl buttons.
German, 1890–93
Given by the National Westminster Bank
T.778-1972

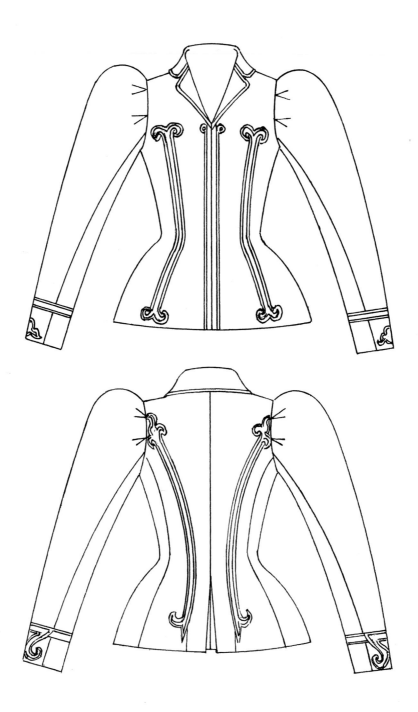

Traditionally tailoring was largely reserved for men's coats. Riding habits were one of the few women's garments available in a tailored style. Gradually demand grew for stylish, practical and hard-wearing outfits suitable for a wide range of outdoor activities including shopping, travelling and walking. By the 1870s the tailored look for women had really begun to take hold. Cutting systems used on men's suits were transferred to fashionable skirts and bodices and the resulting styles were rapidly adopted. Fashion magazines and cutting journals trumpeted the superior skill of the tailor, whose methods of manipulating cloth captured the full beauty of the female form.

This bodice shows how the tailor has modified his techniques to suit the fashionable silhouette. With special attention to measuring, cutting and making he has moulded the cloth to follow the curves of the bust, hollow of the waist and prominence of the hips. The outer cloth was fitted to the figure with the aid of a canvas interlining constructed with darts and seams to give the required contours. Both were skilfully pressed into shape using a variety of irons and a damp rag which was necessary to produce steam. The rich colour and luxurious velvet decoration heightens the jacket's feminine appeal, which is capped by full sleeves in true 1890s style.

Woman's jacket bodice (with matching skirt) made of superfine trimmed with velvet and braid.
Lined with canvas, silk and whalebone strips.
British, about 1895
Given by Miss N. Harrison
T.173-1969

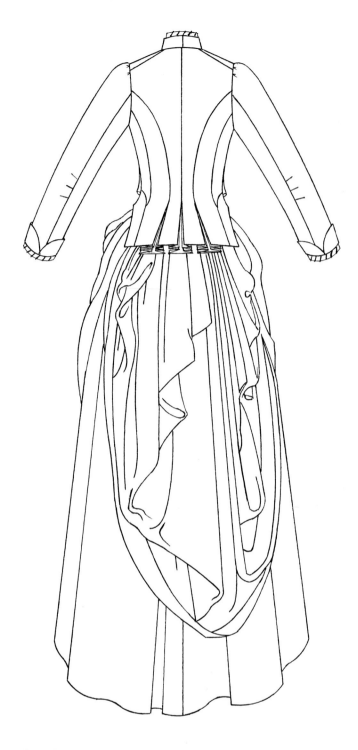

This tailor-made bustle dress could have stepped off the pages of a fashion magazine. In 1885 bodices incorporating collars and lapels in the style of men's jackets became a popular novelty. They were cut to wear open in front revealing an underbodice which resembled a man's waistcoat. In this example the underbodice is attached to the outer jacket at the side seam. This was usual as it helped the bodice sit into the form of the body while retaining the appearance of a separate jacket and fancy waistcoat. Such outfits made elegant walking costumes, suitable for a fashionable shopping street or a promenade in the park.

By this date the bustle was at its height, projecting from the back of the dress while the front remained comparatively flat. The overskirts were caught up in a profusion of pleats, draperies and puffings to create interesting effects and emphasize the silhouette. This ensemble has steel hoops and tapes inserted into the back of the underskirt to pull it into the required shape over a bustle pad. Despite these contrivances, the hem would have just reached the top of the shoes, making it more practical for walking than a trained skirt.

For more information on this outfit see page 212.

Bodice and skirt made of wool and silk.
Madame Cridon, Robes & Confections. Paris, 1885
T.715-1997

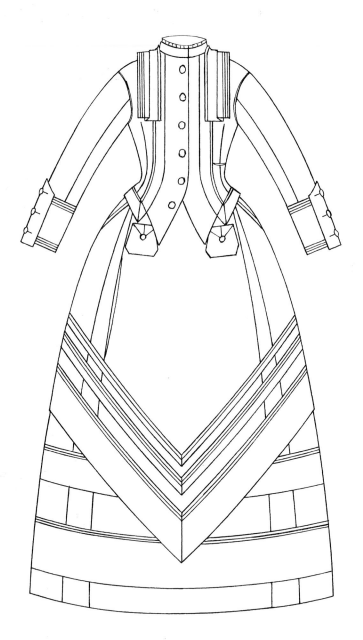 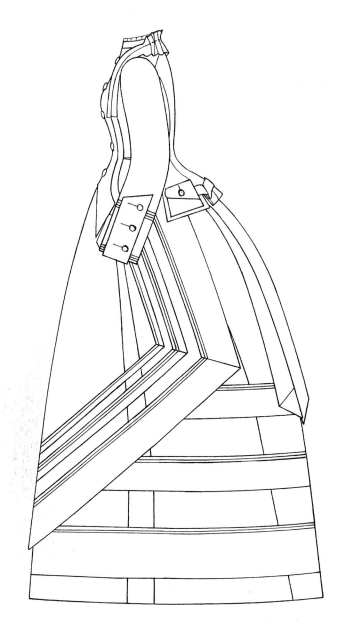

This sailor-style outfit conjures up images of holidays by the sea. In Britain the expansion of the railways and rising middle-class prosperity meant that coastal towns such as Brighton, Scarborough and Torquay became increasingly popular destinations, and fashion amply catered for the tastes in jaunty summer wear. Charming dresses in lively stripes, colourful chintzes and cool muslins enlivened the esplanades, as women donned their seaside wardrobes.

Blue and white stripes, deep cuffs, indigo linen bands decorating the skirt and neat rows of applied braid give this dress a nautical air. It is derived from the sailor suit popularized for fashionable wear by the Prince of Wales (Edward VII, 1841–1910) in 1846. His outfit was based on the dress of the crew of the royal yacht, with its large sailor collar, bell-bottom trousers and knotted neckerchief. Soon parents were dressing their children in similar designs and women gradually appropriated the 'Jack Tar' image for themselves.[1]

As well as displaying maritime traits, this style of dress was more comfortable and practical than many fashions. Made of sturdy cotton and linen it would be cooler and more hard-wearing than silk. The bodice is not boned which was a big concession in the 1870s, although a corset would still be worn underneath. Sensible yet stylish, it was ideal for genteel excursions or a stroll along the front, especially when topped with a dainty straw hat.

1. 'Jack Tar' was an informal name for a sailor. An official uniform for naval ratings was introduced in 1857. Before this date seamen wore a mixture of clothes, although naval captains tried to keep their ship's companies looking similar and smart.

Seaside costume, bodice and skirt. Made of cotton trimmed with linen and applied silk braid and bone buttons. Fastened with hooks and eyes.
British, 1872
Given by Miss Julia Reckitt and Messrs G. F. & A. I. Reckitt
T.128-1923

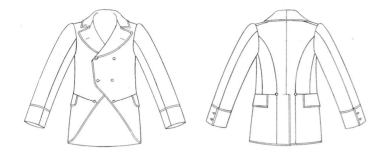

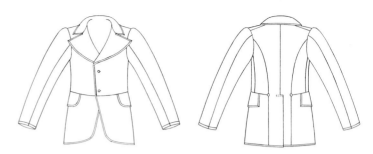

A distinctive feature of this coat is the angled forepart sloping away from the second button. This style of morning coat was fashionable during the early 1870s and was known as the 'University' or 'Angle-fronted' coat. Black and blue were popular colours and they were made in a variety of cloth, including meltons, velvets, angolas and tweeds. Bold and fancy checks were in favour with 'fast' young gentlemen who often teamed the coats with equally flamboyant trousers.

Double-breasted versions required skilful tailoring, particularly as they were usually fastened on one or two buttons. Many men wanted the coats as angled as possible to reveal colourful waistcoats and gold watch chains at the waist. It was difficult to preserve the double-breasted form, show a portion of the waistcoat and retain a light and elegant appearance. The positioning of the buttons was also critical, for if the tailor did not place them at different distances from the front edge of the coat, it would look clumsy and heavy.

Double-breasted man's morning coat made of velveteen edged with wool braid.
British, 1870–75
Given by Miss M. Leach
T.3-1982

During the latter part of the nineteenth century, fashionable men wore three main styles of coat during the day: the morning coat, frock coat and lounge jacket. The morning coat became popular for business wear and was made in a range of styles to suit the occasion. This example is typical of early 1870s tailoring with its wide lapels, slanting foreparts, flapped pockets in the waist seam, full sleeves and braided edges.

The collar and lapels are cut very low, creating ample opportunity for the wearer to display a fine silk cravat secured with a decorative pin. This style was worn during all seasons and men were encouraged to endure any discomfort from the cold for the sake of fashion. In 1875, however, *The Gentleman's Magazine of Fashion* reported: 'Medical men ascribe many deaths during the past winter to the fashion of low collars and to gentlemen not being sufficiently protected by their clothing at the throat and neck.'

Man's single-breasted morning coat made of superfine edged with wool braid and a velvet collar.
British, 1870–75
T.5-1982

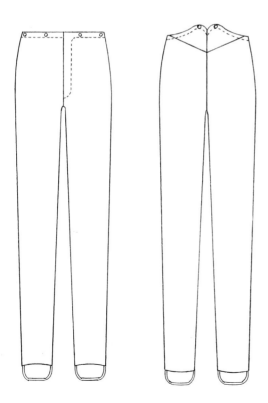

Checked, plain and striped trousers were fashionable attire with morning coats (see above). Stripes were particularly popular as they gave the appearance of extra height, especially if they were cut fairly straight to the ankle. They were, however, difficult to cut correctly as the stripes had to run straight down the leg and match at the seams. This added to the complication of cutting a trouser pattern which would suit the customer and fit well whether standing, walking or sitting. In this example the tailor has positioned the fabric on the bias to give sufficient room for the seat while cleverly matching the stripes in an inverted 'V' shape. The bias given to the seat seam was known as the 'seat angle'. Two rising points cut in the top at the centre back accommodate the brace buttons which are stamped with 'E. Parkin & Sons, Sheffield'. Less care has been taken to align the fabric here, possibly because it was concealed under the coat.

Man's trousers (back view) of wool woven with a diagonal stripe, part lined with cotton.
British, 1870–80
T.118-1953

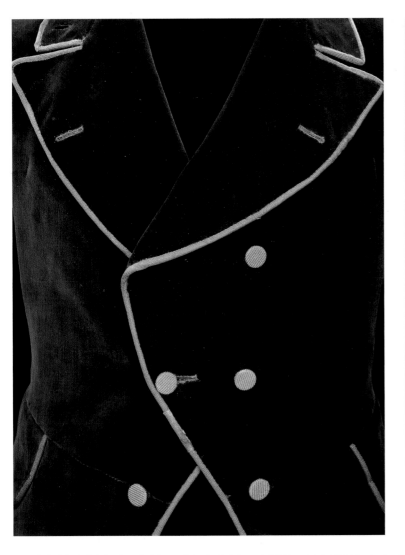

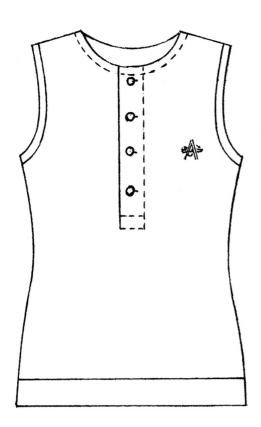

Blue and orange stripes give a vibrant splash of colour to this fully-fashioned silk vest. Teamed with matching pants sporting a grey silk waistband, it would have formed a striking feature of any man's wardrobe. The embroidered coronet and initials 'M.A.' suggest that it belonged to Henry Cyril Paget, the Fifth Marquis of Anglesey (1875–1905).

The Marquis was a flamboyant character who let his fantasies run wild after inheriting the family estates and marrying his beautiful cousin, Lilian Florence Maud, in 1898. Within a few weeks he had amassed a remarkable collection of jewellery, bedecking his wife in emeralds and diamonds and mortgaging his estates in the process. Shortly afterwards Lily left him and he immersed himself in theatricals, staging productions and earning the nickname of the 'Dancing Marquis' for his performance of

'the Butterfly Dance'. The costs incurred were enormous and eventually his creditors caught up with him and the Marquis was declared bankrupt in 1904, dying of pleurisy a year later at the age of thirty.[1]

When not on the stage, the Marquis was a very elegant dresser, procuring the finest tailored suits and accessories. He acquired this vest from 'Doucet Jeune', one of the best men's shirtmaking establishments in Paris, which had outlets in Chicago, New York and London. A cousin of Jacques Doucet (1853–1929), the famous Paris couturier, built up this business during the 1870s.

1. Copyright to reproduce this information given by kind permission of Christopher Simon Sykes, author of *The Visitors' Book* (Hull, 1990).

A man's machine-knitted silk vest with mother of pearl buttons.
Doucet Jeune. Paris, 1890–1905
Given by Mr and Mrs John Leathwood
T.89-2003

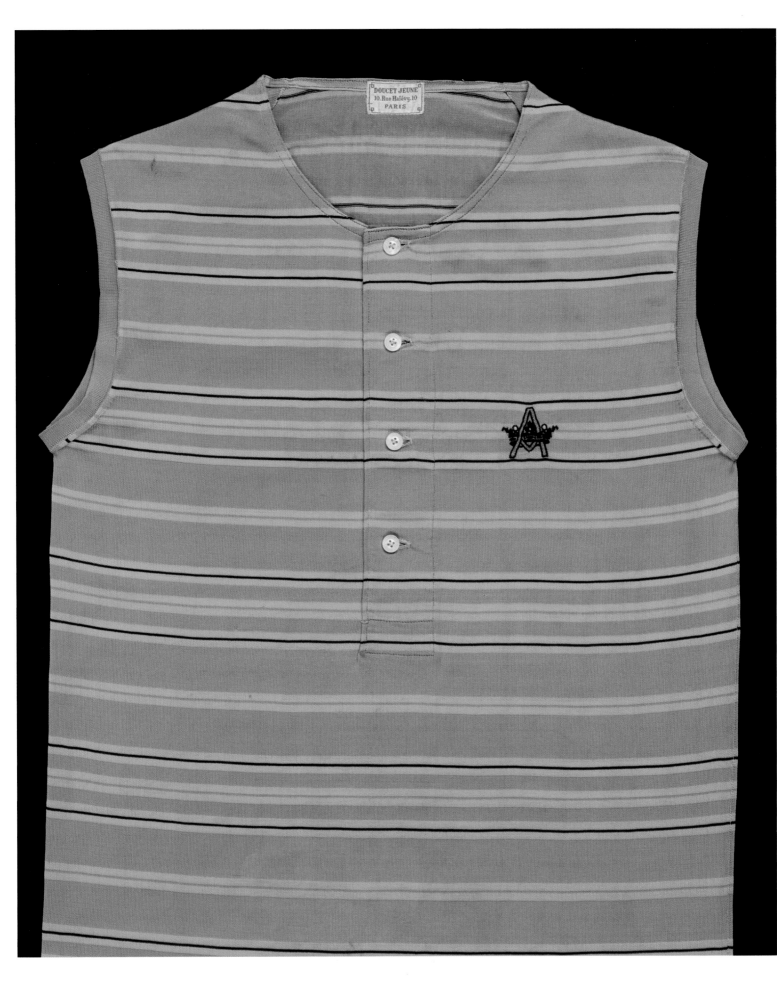

An embroidered jackal or fox races across the collar of this linen coat. Jackal-hunting was popular among British soldiers and administrators living in India during the nineteenth century. The rules were based on the British fox-hunt, although the hunting packs tended to be made up of dogs of different breeds known as 'Bobbery-packs' in Anglo-Indian colloquial terms, hence the name 'Bobbery Hunt'.[1]

This light linen coat would have proved ideal for hot climates, replacing the heavy woollen cloth used for British hunts. It was probably worn by the huntsman who looked after the dogs, as the slanting pocket on the front could have held a hunting whistle or horn. The collar is very similar to one worn by the Earl of Darlington for a Yorkshire hunt in 1826: 'Lady Arabella was attired in her scarlet habit, and his Lordship in a straight-cut scarlet coat, with an embroidered fox on the collar, a hat, and a leather girdle across his shoulder. His two whippers-in were also in hats, and had the embroidered fox on the collar.'[2]

1. 'Bobbery-pack, A pack of hounds of different breeds, or (oftener) of no breed at all … wherewith young officers hunt jackals or the like.' Colonel Henry Yule, *A Glossary of Anglo-Indian Colloquial Words and Phrases* (London, 1886), p.76.

2. C.J. Apperley (Nimrod), *Nimrod's Hunting Tours – Nimrod's Yorkshire Tour, 1826* (reprinted 1933), p.201.

Man's coat of unbleached linen, velvet collar embroidered with metal thread couched with linen. Trimmed with silk cord and fastened with velvet-covered buttons.
Anglo-Indian, 1800–20
Given by Messrs Harrods Ltd
T.742-1913

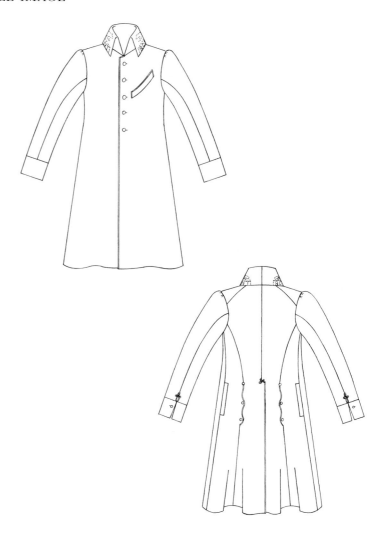

The possibility of bad weather and rough terrain on a hunt meant that clothing needed to be wind- and water-resistant. The underside of this collar is fitted with a buttoned tab (known as a kidney), which would have provided some protection against the elements. The button farthest from view could be undone and the collar placed across the chin and fastened to a button on the other side to keep out the wind and rain. In more clement weather, the collar could be pressed flat to create lapels. The rows of padding stitches visible at the neckline secure the canvas interlining in place, helping to stiffen the collar and mould it into shape.

Frock coats were better suited to hunting than cutaway tail-coats as the fuller skirts gave a better covering for the upper leg. Surtees' character Mr Jorrocks was well aware of their benefits and declared, 'there's nothin' like room and flannel; good long-backed coats, with the waistcoat made equally warm all round, and the back to come down in a flap, and plenty of good well-lined laps to wrap over one's thighs when it rains'.[1]

For more information on this coat see page 36.

1. R.S. Surtees, *Handley Cross* (London, 1854), p.319.

Man's hunting frock coat of superfine fastened with gilt brass buttons.
Surrey Stag Hounds. Buttons made by Pitt & Co., 50 St Martin's Lane, London. English, 1860–1900
Given by Messrs Harrods Ltd
T.770-1913

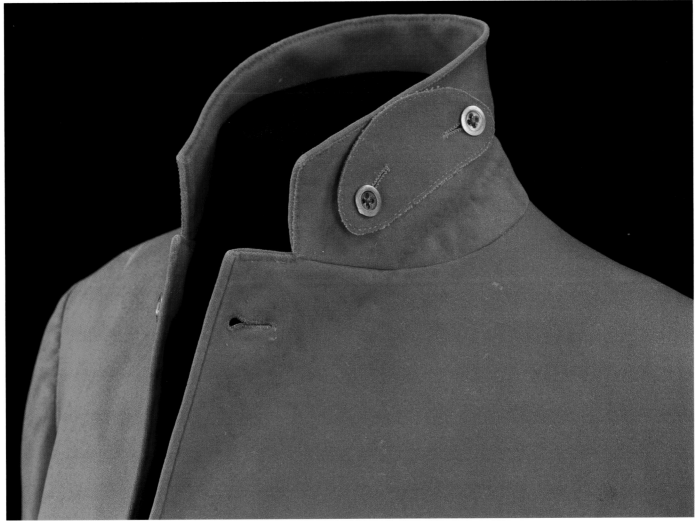

This coat was clearly designed for shooting. Four buttons depicting popular outdoor pursuits such as deer-stalking fasten the front, and one of the centre back buttons illustrates a pair of hounds. The flapped breast pockets might have held cartridges or a powder flask and the large pockets in the waist-seam, percussion caps. Two capacious pockets placed across the inside skirt are known as 'poacher's' or 'hare' pockets as they were large enough to carry dead game. *The Tailor and Cutter* of 7 August 1869 reported that many gentlemen objected to too many pockets. So as to avoid unnecessary weight they preferred to carry their necessaries in a small bag on their backs and in an ammunition pouch fastened to a small waist-belt. A well-cut pair of knickerbockers, gaiters and hat would have completed the outfit.

Man's shooting jacket of velveteen fastened with gilt
brass buttons.
British, 1869–80
Bequeathed by Mr E. W. Mynott
T.76-1980

A stag's head and antlers encircle the initials S.S.H. on these hunt buttons. This was the emblem of the Surrey Stag Hounds. Engraved buttons were expensive and these are firmly attached to the coat with a metal shank and circle of fabric for extra protection and reinforcement.

Stag-hunting was a popular sport during the Middle Ages and Tudor period. By the nineteenth century it had been eclipsed by fox-hunting due to shortage of deer and agricultural change. Despite this, packs such as the Queen's Hounds and the Surrey Stag Hounds sustained its prestige. The clothing was similar to that worn for hunting foxes and consisted of a scarlet coat, black hat, breeches, top-boots and spurs. Lord Ribblesdale, master of the Queen's Buckhounds between 1892 and 1895, was a stickler for sartorial correctness and stated, '*de rigueur* hunting dress must be very well done or not done at all'.[1]

For more information on this coat see page 34.

1. Lord Ribblesdale, Master of the Buckhounds 1892–95, *The Queen's Hounds and Stag-Hunting Recollections* (London, 1897), p.157.

Man's coat of superfine with brass buttons.
Surrey Stag Hounds. Buttons made by Pitt & Co., 50 St Martin's Lane, London. English, 1860–1900
Given by Messrs Harrods Ltd
T.770-1913

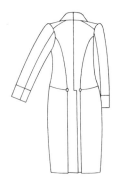

The initials H.H. are emblazoned on the buttons of this elegant evening coat, showing that the wearer belonged to the Hampshire Hunt. He would have been a paying member, contributing towards the cost of the hunt. This entitled him to attend meets and also social functions such as hunt dinners and balls.

The paying of subscriptions marked a fundamental change in the history of fox-hunting. In the eighteenth century hunting was a largely private affair, organized and funded by single aristocrats or select clubs. By 1860 social change and the extension of the railways had opened up the sport to a wider section of society. To cover increasing expenses, most hunts were now organized as subscription packs. A gentleman, regardless of where he lived, could become a member. The buttons were an emblem of his acceptance into the pack.

For more information on this coat see page 138.

Man's dress coat, made of superfine with gilt brass buttons.
Hampshire Hunt. Buttons made by Firmin & Sons, 153 Strand, London. English, 1860–1900
Given by Harry Helman
T.373-1990

During the late eighteenth and early nineteenth centuries there was a revival of archery in Britain. The numbers of societies rapidly increased and with them the regulations governing dress. Many publications offered advice on what to wear, including *The Bijou Book of Out-Door Amusements*, which stated that, 'The dress of the archer varies in different clubs … For gentlemen, nothing is better than a green cloth coat with gilt buttons, having the club device upon them.'[1] These buttons are engraved with an arrow and show that the wearer belonged to the Walton Le Dale archery club, Lancashire.

For shooting, a green jacket was recommended as this is the colour traditionally associated with archery.[2] As well as headwear, breeches, boots and equipment, men often had to invest in outfits for different occasions. This coat is cut in the style of court dress, suggesting it was worn for ceremonial events. Archery could therefore be a costly sport, especially as fines could be imposed for not wearing the prescribed uniform.

1. *The Bijou Book of Out-Door Amusements* (London, 1868), pp59–61.
2. The tradition supposedly originates from medieval foresters and huntsmen who wore the colour as a form of camouflage.

Man's archery court dress coat of broadcloth with gilt brass buttons.
English, 1830–50
Given by Mrs Katherine Rachel Thomas née Gorst. Acquired with a collection of costume worn by members of the Lowndes family, formerly of Leahall, Chesterfield, and the Gorst family of Chester
Circ.108-1963

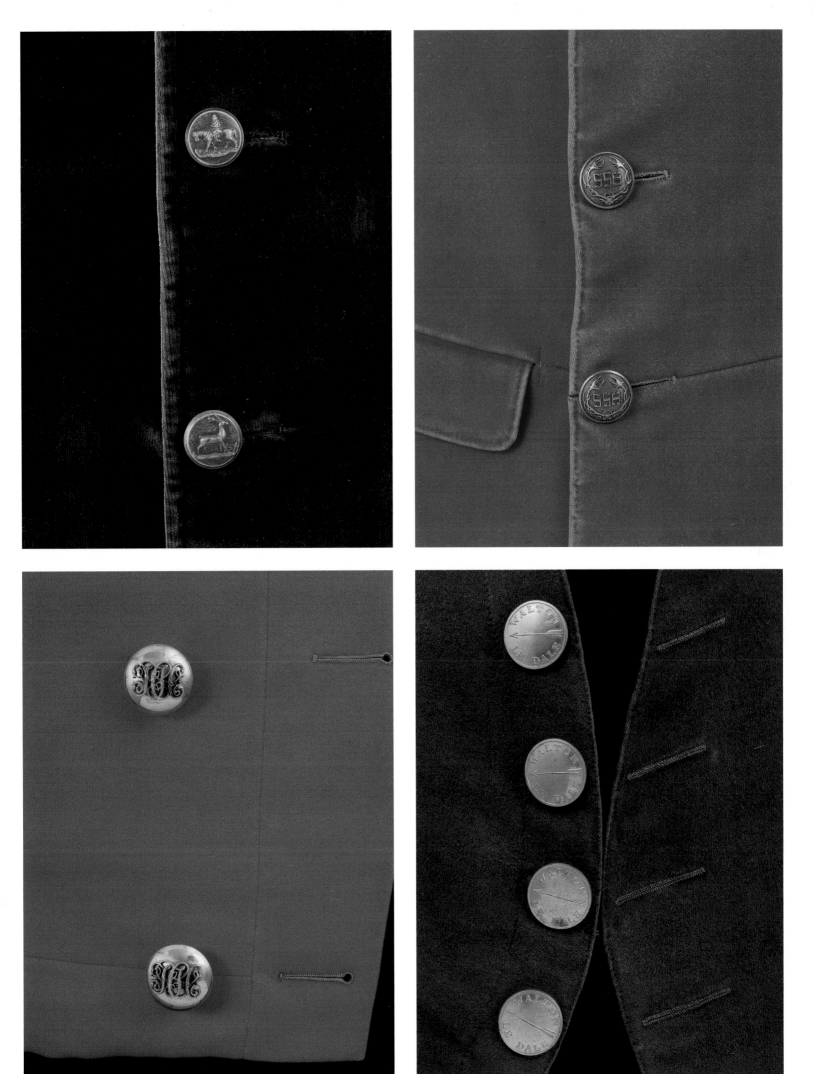

Historicism

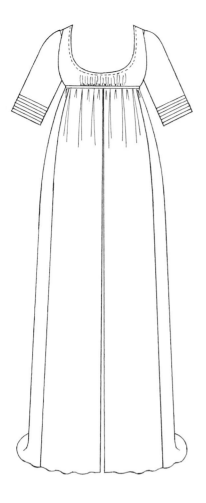

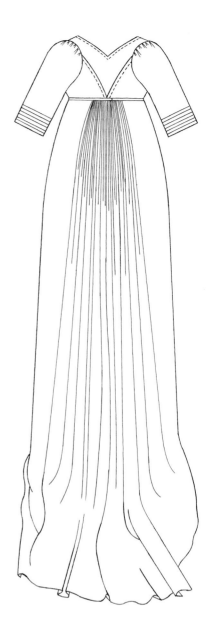

This gown epitomizes neo-classical style in dress with its high waistline, diaphanous fabric and flowing skirt. The Classical revival so apparent in architecture did not really make its mark on fashion until about 1795, when high-waisted white gowns imitating Greek and Roman garments became popular. This dress shares a similar reverence for antiquity through its simple lines and linear silhouette.

A plain underdress is worn beneath for modesty and to illuminate the delicate floral pattern on the muslin. Very fine Indian muslins and cottons were popular for this style of gown as the fabric draped in an appropriately 'classical' manner. As they were often embroidered in India for the European market, the designs did not always reflect classical decorative motifs. In this example, scrolling leaves and tendrils wind their way down the bodice and skirt instead of classical motifs, giving the dress a less formal appeal.

Also of Indian origin were the shawls that often complemented these simple gowns. They functioned as a light wrap and emphasized the neo-classical look when draped around the shoulders or arms. Kashmirs imported from northern India were the most highly prized shawls and inspired British and French imitations. Here, the basic design layout, with its plain centre and deep borders, is very similar to a genuine Kashmir shawl. However, the delicate bell-shaped flowers in place of the traditional Kashmiri 'buta'[1] or 'pine' motif, as well as the choice of colour, give it a distinctly European character.

1. Flower or bush.

Muslin gown embroidered in cotton thread (the silk underdress is a replica).
Fabric: Indian. Gown: British, about 1800
Given by Messrs Harrods Ltd
T.785-1913

Shawl of silk twill with brocaded pattern woven in silk.
Possibly Spitalfields. London, 1801–11
Given by Miss C. G. Wigginton
T.213-1996

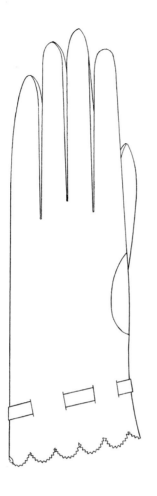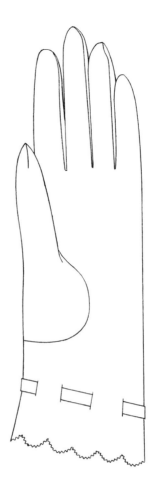

This fashionable and highly decorative glove of rich cream kid reflects the trend for neo-classicism which epitomized dress in the early part of the nineteenth century. Printed gloves of this style were fashionable in England and throughout Europe but are said to have originated in Spain. This fine example is of Spanish origin, as can be seen by the caption underneath the image: 'Venus y las tres Gracias'. The image depicts Venus and the three Graces (Thalia, Aglaia and Euphrosine) together with Cupid. In the foreground can be seen two turtle doves, the attributes of Venus, and a quiver and bow, the attributes of Cupid. The story is taken from Greek mythology and the legend of the love affair between Mars, the god of war, and Venus, the goddess of love. It corresponds to the idea that beauty and love will disarm and triumph over force.

The glove illustrated is a homage to and symbolic of love. Throughout the seventeenth, eighteenth and early nineteenth centuries it was the custom to give gloves on many social occasions. Etiquette decreed that gloves were one of the few gifts which a gentleman could with propriety present to a lady who was not his wife.

The pattern of the glove is cut with 'quirks' and 'fourchettes', but there are no 'points' as the backs were left plain in order to accommodate the printed and hand-coloured design. An elegant border depicting myrtle, the symbol of love and also an attribute of Venus, runs around the wrist. A threaded, madder-dyed pink ribbon completes the applied decoration. The cuff is scalloped and pinked to give added refinement and delicacy to the design of the glove.
M. K.

Woman's glove of cream kid with a neo-classical design printed in black and hand-coloured.
Spanish, 1800–20
Given by Messrs Harrods Ltd
T.639-1913

VENUS Y LAS TRES GRACIAS.

Ivory coloured silks billow out in four openings at the top of the sleeves of this dress. These puffed trimmings are inspired by the fashionable slashing of garments in the Renaissance period when the top fabric was cut to reveal a coloured lining or garment. Here, a long rectangular strip of ivory silk is stitched to the inside of the sleeve head and the excess gathered into puffs through the openings. The nineteenth-century version of slashing is much more controlled by cut, stitching and piped edges, rather than the raw cuts in fabric seen in the sixteenth century.

Made of vibrant canary yellow silk, this dress emphasizes the neo-classical vertical line by the use of a high waist which produces a disproportionately long skirt. Another historically inspired trimming appears around the lower hem of the skirt in the applied so-called vandyked border of ivory silk. The long sleeves are narrow at the wrists, with double bands at the cuffs and trimmed with ivory silk satin frills, yellow silk crêpe, cream ribbon and cording.
H. P.

Dress of yellow silk with ivory silk decoration.
British, c.1810
Given by Sydney Vacher, Esq.
T.8-1918

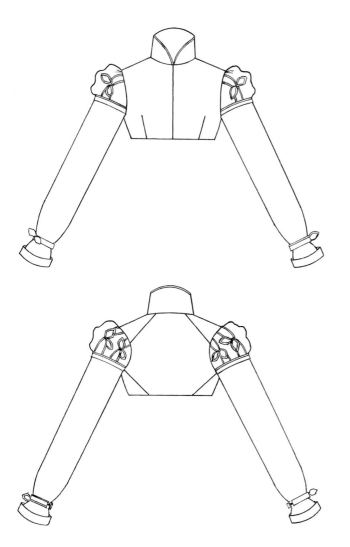

The high-waisted spencer was initially a man's garment. It is said to have originated in the late 1790s and took its name from George, the second Earl Spencer (1758–1834). The practical features of this outer garment meant that it soon came to be appreciated by women as well, as it kept the cold at bay when wearing the fashionable thin muslin dresses. It was worn with walking dress until the mid-1820s.

The high stand collar and short puffed oversleeves trimmed with satin-faced matching bows signal the popularity of the 'Gothic' influence on early nineteenth-century female costume. Elements from dress of the twelfth to sixteenth centuries were constantly borrowed and later termed as *le style troubadour*.

A rich, dark blue velvet has been used in the spencer shown here. It is lined with linen throughout and fastens edge to edge at the front with hooks and eyes. The long sleeves are fastened with wrist bands and trimmed in a similar way to the oversleeves.
H. P.

Spencer of blue velvet.
British, c.1818
Given by Messrs Harrods Ltd
T.890-1913

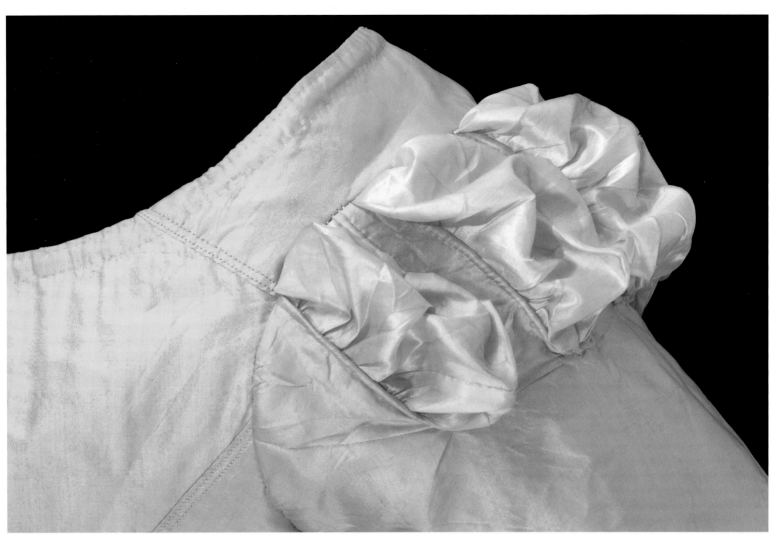

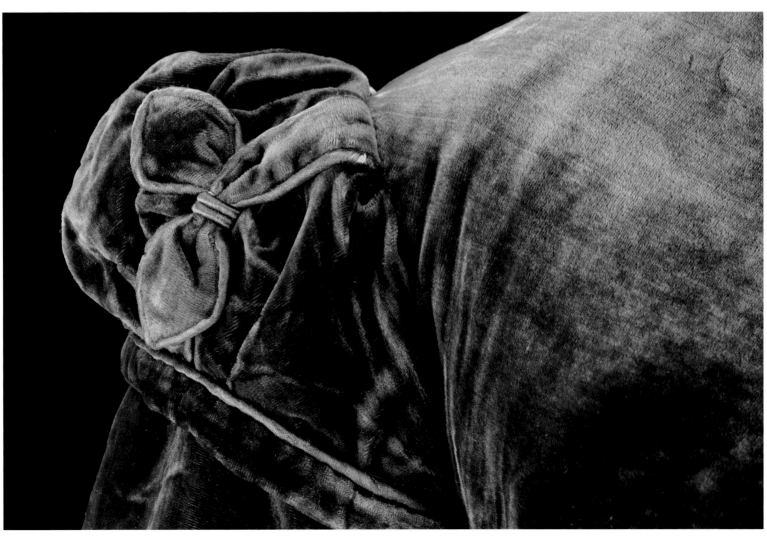

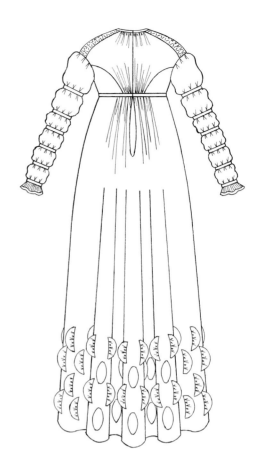

During the early years of the nineteenth century, Greek and Roman influences on dress remained strong. Long, white muslin gowns with high waists were loosely based on the simple tunics featured in classical art. Soon, however, a taste for greater ornamentation began to interrupt the purity of the neo-classical line. So-called 'Gothic' styles inspired by Medieval, Tudor, Elizabethan and seventeenth-century costume flourished in British dress, and puffs of fabric, slashed decoration, elaborate ruffs, vandyked borders and names such as the 'Medici' collar and 'Marie' sleeve reveal a fascination with history.

With its white muslin and puffed decoration, this dress is a hybrid of historical influences. As with most garments of this period, it is not possible to pinpoint exactly where each detail comes from, as they are often fanciful interpretations of past styles. By looking at portraiture and studying contemporary descriptions of fashion, however, it is possible to trace similar elements of design.

The general shape of this example follows on from neo-classical models with its raised waistline and soft, clinging fabric. The antique statue effect is mitigated by the flared skirt which falls from the waist in a triangular line as opposed to the tubular silhouette of earlier dress. Four rows of muslin puffs are stitched and gathered to the bottom of the skirt. These are reminiscent of decoration on Tudor dress, where the sleeves or doublet were often slashed and the undershirt drawn through the openings to form a series of puffs. Soft bands of muslin catch the sleeves into delicate *bouffants* in the style of seventeenth-century dress. A ruff or frill of lace would probably have been worn at the neck to add to the sense of romantic nostalgia.

Introduced in about 1816, this type of decoration was widely adopted and long lasting. As late as November 1824 the fashion magazine *Ackermann's Repository* depicted a similar white dress, 'with a gold embroidered trimming *à l'antique*, and a narrow tucker of fine blonde: the front is also embroidered with gold, in the form of a stomacher; and a gold embroidered band round the waist corresponds with the bands that confine the long full sleeves, which are arranged in seven *bouffants* …The skirt has an elegant trimming composed of three tucks … beneath (which) is a *bouilonné* of *barège*.'

Dress decorated with muslin puffs and reed-smocking.
British, 1816–21
Given by Miss C .L. Buckle
T.55-1934

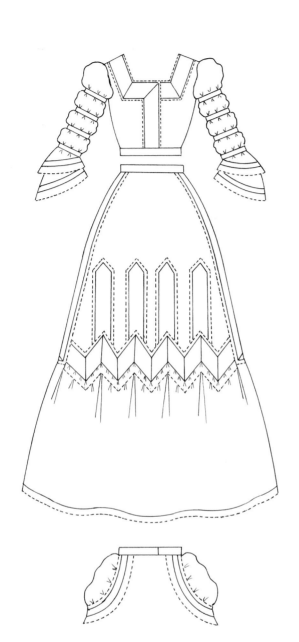

Puffs of linen lawn interspersed with bands of silk satin and lace give this sleeve a filmy, weightless quality. They are reminiscent of the puffings on 1620s gowns which swelled out above and below the elbow, confined at intervals by ribbons. This device had been used throughout the nineteenth century in one form or another, but it suited the light fabrics of 1860s summer dresses particularly well. It also complemented the fashionable 'pannier-style' skirts, which were looped, gathered or drawn up with strings into back and side puffs.

The sleeve is cleverly constructed to create the impression of gossamer without losing its shape. It is made from a piece of linen lawn gathered into a series of puffs which are sewn into position on the underside of the ribbon bands. Inside each puff four pieces of cord are held in place with stitches to maintain the correct tension. These are just visible through the transparent fabric and give the illusion that the puffs have been drawn up like a roman blind. To complete the harmony, two frills trimmed with ribbon and lace delicately curve over the wrist and hand.

Bodice made of linen lawn trimmed with silk-satin ribbon overlaid with
Maltese-style bobbin lace, probably Bedfordshire (the silk undersleeve is a replica).
British, about 1868
Given by Miss Ada B. Cooper
T.13-1943

A striped eighteenth-century silk gives this dress a vibrant quality. Women's clothes were often made from earlier fabrics, particularly when the colours, pattern and texture suited the fashions of the day. Eighteenth-century taffetas were popular during the 1820s and 1830s as these crisp silks helped the skirts stand away from the body in graceful folds and the sleeves billow into elegant puffs. The delicate floral designs, woven stripes and soft colours also complemented contemporary tastes in dress.

This evening gown is made from silk tobine dating from the 1770s. Silk tobines were taffetas patterned by being woven with an extra warp floating on the surface that was bound at intervals with silk weft threads. The warp here is in shades of red and the pattern it creates helps break up the uniformity of the stripes. This fabric was probably selected because, from a distance, the yellow, pink and red stripes resemble the 'rainbow style' prints introduced in the 1820s. 'Rainbow style' was a method of block-printing invented by the paper-stainer Spoerlin of Vienna. It was the first block-printed style adapted for roller-printing, as after the colours were applied to the cloth they were merged at the edges using a brush or roller. The result was a soft blending of colours evoking the effects of a rainbow.

Evening dress made of woven silk tobine trimmed with silk satin and lined with cotton.
British, silk: 1770s; dress: 1827–29
Given by Miss C. Granger-Evans
T.1-1967

Pink and mauve floral sprigs powder the bodice and skirt of this evening dress. Soft tones and delicate patterns were popular, and eighteenth-century silks like this one proved ideal for creating harmonious effects. Stitch marks on the skirt and bodice show where the original 1770s gown has been unpicked and the applied decoration removed. It was quite common for clothes to be taken apart and remodelled to suit the latest styles. Crisp silks like this one were perfect for making the long, fitted bodices and full skirts fashionable during the 1840s. It was also much cheaper to restyle an old dress than buy a new silk of this quality.

Small tubular pleats known as 'organ pleats' gather the fabric into the waist of this dress. They were often used during this period to give an even fullness to the skirt, helping it fall away from the body in graceful folds. Organ pleats also accentuated the deep point of the bodice. This one is very long and is supported by four pieces of whalebone inserted into the lining at the centre front seam and darts. The rigid structure and precise fit would have held the body in a stiff, unnatural position, aided by the corset worn underneath.

Evening dress of Spitalfields brocaded silk. Bodice lined with cotton and whalebone strips.
British, silk: 1770s; altered: 1840s
Given by Mrs C. Shaw
T.854-1974

The copious folds of this greatcoat proved ideal for keeping a gentleman warm outdoors, especially when riding. It would have been worn over at least one coat and the tailor has allowed for this in the generous cut. The waist, chest and sleeves are particularly roomy, giving the wearer freedom of choice in his dress and ease of movement. The tailor has also ensured that the ample skirts are very long, covering the knees and much of the calf for extra protection.

Like most early nineteenth-century coats, there are distinct references to former styles of tailoring. The hip buttons, positioned on either side of the centre back vent, are inherited from the end of the seventeenth century. They serve as ornamental headings to the back pleats which resemble the sword vents on eighteenth-century coats. Two vertical flaps known as 'skirt pockets' project from the folds of these pleats, fastened with buttons to discourage pickpockets.

Man's greatcoat of superfine, pockets lined with linen.
British, about 1810
Given by Revd J. P. Bushell and Mr Anthony Bushell
T.86-1959

The seams on the back of this dress are close together on the shoulders and almost meet at the waist, forming a diamond shape. This gives the appearance of a very small back, emphasized by the oversleeves which are set extremely far in. This cut was very fashionable during the early 1800s as it complemented the simple lines of the high-waisted dresses and created a slender-bodied look. It was also a continuation of the 'tight-back' style fashionable during the eighteenth century.

Inverted pleats at the centre back give shape and fullness to the skirt. A small roll or pad was often attached under the back of the dress to create a subtle roundness and to help the fabric hang in fan-like folds. This contrasts with the front of the skirt which is made up of a single width of fabric which falls straight to the ground. The excess material is not gathered but pulled towards the back with strings, rather like a wraparound skirt.

Woman's dress of woven silk with applied plaited trimming. Lined with linen.
British, about 1805
T.188-1921

Soft flutes of silk are worked with smocking stitches on the back of this dress. The style is typical of 1890s Liberty gowns with their loose cut, puffed sleeves and draping fabrics in muted shades of fine 'art' silk. They appealed to increasing numbers of Englishwomen who aspired to dress artistically and sought alternatives to the stiff materials and tight-fitting bodices of conventional dress. Many Liberty garments were boned, however, suggesting that although they looked unrestrictive they would have been worn over corsets. In this example there are three vertical whalebone supports stitched onto the lining at the back, two on each side and five at the front.

'Liberty & Co, Artistic and Historic Costume Studio, 222 Regent St, W.' is printed onto the waist-tape which fastens around the waist inside the garment. This refers to the dress department which opened in 1884 under the guidance of the Aesthetic designer E.W. Godwin (1833–86). Godwin argued that true beauty must be found in the past and flowing styles based on historical originals became a key feature of Liberty designs. Their catalogues illustrate gowns inspired by Greek, Medieval,

Regency and early Victorian fashions with contemporary modifications, and the example here is similar to a style depicted in the 1893 catalogue which echoes high-waisted gowns from 'the palmy days of the First Empire (1804–1814)'.[1]

The smocked decoration at the waist is mirrored in details on the sleeves and cuffs. Smocking was a prominent feature of many Liberty designs and appeared on children's clothes as well as ladies' blouses, jackets and tea gowns and dresses. It was traditionally a rural skill and *The Woman's World* of 1890 describes how 'when the fashionable revival of this difficult craft began … the artistic modistes had to send their delicate "Liberty" silks down to humble cottages in this county (Sussex) and in Dorsetshire where a few conservative rustics still adhere to the old smock-frock.'[2]

1. *Evolution in Costume illustrated by Past Fashion Plates and Present Adaptations of the Empire and the Early Victorian Period Compiled and Invented by Messrs Liberty London and Paris 1893*, Modification of Example VII. (see p.22 *The Empire Mode*, Modification of Example VII).
2. Barbara Morris, *Liberty Design* (Pyramid, London, 1989), p.45.

Dress made of pongee silk, decorated with smocking and trimmed with machine lace. Lined with silk, cotton and whalebone strips.
Liberty & Co. London, 1893–95
Given by Mrs J. D. F. H. Cantrell
T.17-1985

During the 1860s the fashionable skirt became flatter in front with the fullness receding towards the back. Women still wore hooped petticoats (crinolines) to give the desired silhouette, but they were no longer bell-shaped and by 1868 they curved out behind forming a kind of bustle. In order to fall gracefully over these new structures, skirts tended to be gored, that is constructed with triangular panels rather than straight widths of fabric. The striped green skirt in this example is composed of eight gores that significantly reduce the amount of bulky pleating and gathering at the waist characterizing earlier styles. Contrary to much speculation in the press, these gores did not radically diminish the size of the skirt as *The Englishwoman's Domestic Magazine* pointed out in March 1868: 'Skirts are gored, it is true, but they are ample and flowing. Crinolines, far from being left off, have merely changed their shape; they are plain in front, but puffed out on either side so as to remind one strongly of the hoops or paniers of the last century.'

This dress follows the vogue for historical revival with its separate draped overskirt loosely based on eighteenth-century polonaise gowns. Some looped-up styles were given nostalgic names such as 'double skirt *à la Watteau*' and '*Marie Antoinette* dress' or were raised with cords and ribbon bows in the style of the originals. The resulting puffs and draperies were copiously trimmed with silk fringe, brocaded satin braid, beads, marabou feathers, garlands and applied silk flowers. Beneath all these layers and decorative trimmings it is a wonder that a woman could discreetly find her watch pocket which was often concealed in the waistband of her skirt.

Day dress (bodice, skirt, overskirt and sash) made of silk woven with a horizontal stripe and trimmed
with braid, beads, hand-made Maltese-style bobbin lace and silk fringe. The bodice is lined with cotton and whalebone strips.
British, 1868
T.37-1984

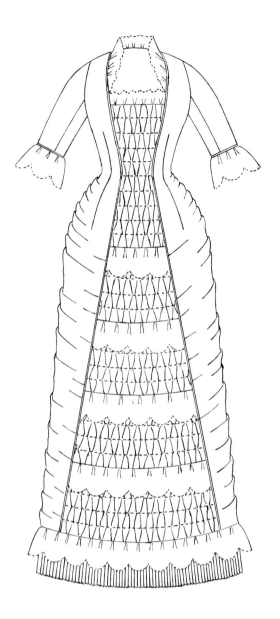

During the late 1870s, fashion moved away from bustled silhouettes to sheath-like dresses that emphasized the shapely curves of the body. Princess dresses[1] suited this style particularly well as the bodice and skirt were cut in one with no seam at the waist. This construction created a long, narrow line and a smooth fit over the contours of the bust and hips, accentuated by the figure-hugging corsets worn beneath. The fitted look was also achieved by cutting the bodice with five seams at the back and inserting front darts that curved in at the waist and then out again (see line drawing). The bodice was often fastened at the centre front, or as in this example, with a concealed hook and eye closure on one side.

Princess dresses became extremely fashionable and this image shows how a profusion of trimmings and lace enhanced their elegant effects. The eye is immediately drawn to the ruched front panel that is shaped to flatter the figure, being wider at the neck and nipped in at the waist. A narrow row of gold piping separates it from the sides of the dress, woven with a sweeping Baroque pattern based on roses and acanthus leaves. This creates the impression of an open gown which was fashionable during the eighteenth century. Historical references are also visible in the square neckline and lace trimming which is supported by wire. These construction details were probably inspired by 1770s 'Rubenesque' dress, which imitated collars and ruffs seen in seventeenth-century portraiture.

1. The Princess dress was first introduced in the 1840s but did not become popular until the 1870s.

Princess evening dress made of jacquard-woven silk and ruched silk
trimmed with machine-lace imitating hand-made blonde silk bobbin lace.
British or French, 1878–80
Given by Miss K. Greaswell
Circ.606-1962

Eighteenth-century style radiates from this elegant creation by Maison Worth. From the 1870s Charles Frederick Worth's (1825–95) fascination with historical dress became an important feature in his designs, which he skilfully translated into contemporary couture. He used references from sketches, historical fashion plates and paintings by artists including Titian, Rembrandt and Gainsborough. The eighteenth century held a particular charm and fabrics, embroidery and open-fronted gowns based on this era became a recurring theme over the ensuing decades.

This bodice shows Worth's interpretation of the 'Directoire' style that came into fashion during the late 1880s. 'Directoire' bodices, coats and gowns were inspired by the 1790s redingote, which was popular for walking and riding and characterized by front-buttoning, a falling collar and wide revers like those on a man's coat. Worth has updated the look through clever use of

cut, colour, texture and trimming. He has also introduced a diaphanous frill cascading over the neck and shoulders which partly conceals the large lapels. This frill is reminiscent of buffons or other neckwear which would have been worn with the eighteenth-century redingote. It also softens the vibrant effects of the pink, evoking Worth's famous 'tulle-clouded' gowns of the 1850s and 1860s which diffused textile and cut.

Instead of fastening at the front, the large striped buttons are purely decorative, echoing a man's double-breasted coat. The edges of the false jacket reveal a cream silk foundation bodice overlaid with fine pleated silk to complement the neck frill. The large wired bow takes the eye back into the world of the late nineteenth century, as this type of sash was a typical feature of fashionable gowns.

For more information about this bodice see page 168.

Woman's bodice made of silk with an integrated ribbon stripe, trimmed with silk chiffon and lined
with silk and whalebone strips. Hand- and machine-sewn
Charles Frederick or Jean-Philippe Worth. Paris, 1890–93
Given by the Comtesse de Tremereuc and possibly worn by her mother
T.366-1960

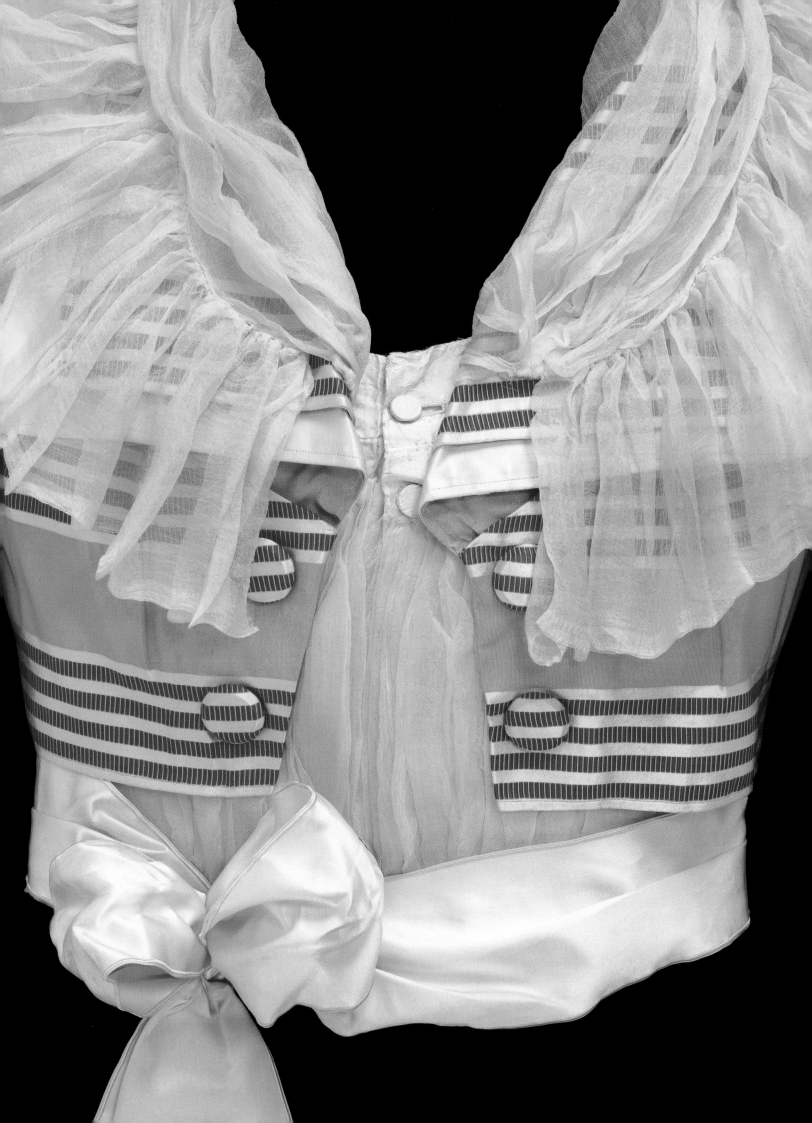

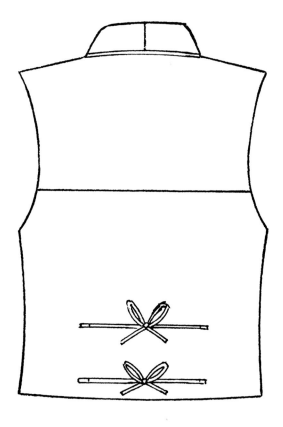

Jousting knights in armour charge across the front of this waist-coat, while black horses, fluttering pennants, pavilion-style tents and heraldic symbols evoke the spirit of a tournament. These motifs reveal aristocratic society's fascination with medieval chivalry during the 1830s and 1840s, when tales of knights provided popular inspiration for decoration.

The scenes on this waistcoat are very similar to those on prints and ceramics depicting the Eglinton Tournament. This extravagant event took place in 1839 on Lord Eglinton's Scottish estate in Ayrshire. The Earl was fired with enthusiasm for chivalry and hoped to recreate every detail of this 'golden age' with pageantry, lavish costumes, authentic props and banqueting tents. Unfortunately, the first two days were severely disrupted by heavy rain, with knights on horseback reduced to cowering under umbrellas!

Despite the weather, the event attracted around 100,000 visitors. A variety of souvenirs were sold to mark the occasion, including buttons, cloaks, headdresses, bonnets, dress-shirts and shawls. The commemorative fabric used to make this waistcoat is similar to fashionable shawl patterns with its harmonious colours and pale ground. The design has been so successfully incorporated into the cut that the lapels, pockets and buttons almost disappear.

Man's waistcoat of woven wool with cotton back and lining.
British, about 1839
Given by Mrs Egidia Haynes
T.129-1969

A variety of passementerie decoration including wrapped buttons, tassels, cord, interlaced designs, fringe and flowers adorn this woman's sleeve. Passementerie is a French term and the collective name given to a wide range of trimmings applied to curtains, cushions and upholstered furniture as well as fashionable dress. Many nineteenth-century designs were based on earlier models. Makers of these trimmings were highly skilled; French manufacturers led the field in innovative technique and imaginative trimmings, while the British followed their styles and adapted them for their own market.

The passementerie trimmings on this sleeve have been cleverly selected to match the colours and the fabric. Pink and green tassels composed of turned wooden balls covered in floss silk and jasmins (loops) harmonize with the jacquard-woven floral pattern. Three-dimensional flower heads of silk wound over card and edged with coiled wire punctuate the design and are reminiscent of ornaments on upholstery fringes. A twisted cord snakes up the centre of the sleeve focusing attention and bringing all the disparate elements of the design together.

Historical references are also visible. The interlaced designs in the centre of this sleeve resemble Celtic knotwork patterns that appear on carved stone crosses, metalwork and illuminated manuscripts in Britain and Ireland. They are formed from three strands of gimp (silk threads wound around a wire or, in this case, cotton core) which are passed alternately over and under one another by hand using a shuttle. The buttons are reminiscent of those on men's eighteenth-century coats, with their glossy threads wound around a domed wooden base to create a pattern. The red, cream and green check could have been inspired by a tartan or coloured checks on fashionable dress silks.

Woman's sleeve made of jacquard-woven silk trimmed with passementerie and lined with silk plush.
British or French, 1845–50
Given by Mrs A. Zamorra and worn by her great grandmother
T.386-1977

A broad band of tartan velvet ribbon decorates the hem, hood and front opening of this woman's cloak. The multi-coloured silk fringe, knotted onto lace, tones in with the colour and symmetry of the woven stripes, creating a charming border. Tartan was frequently used to trim bonnets and mantles as well as cover entire dresses and shawls, reflecting the craze for Highland dress at this time.

Queen Victoria's love of Scotland, her purchase of Balmoral Castle in 1852 and its subsequent rebuilding did a lot to encourage the fashion for tartans. She filled the new castle with tartan: there were carpets in 'Royal Stewart', chairs and sofas in 'Dress Stewart' poplin, and even the draperies in the carriages were made of tartan. Variants of the 'Royal Stewart' tartan included one called 'Victoria', and the Prince Consort designed a sett (pattern) known as the 'Balmoral'.

Cloak of cream wool edged with velvet ribbon, machine lace imitating Chantilly lace and silk fringe. Lined with silk.
British, about 1860
Bequeathed by Mrs M. J. Parsons
T.48-1958

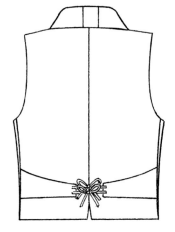

This striking tartan waistcoat would have added a flash of colour to any gentleman's suit. The history of tartan dates back hundreds of years and is clouded in myth and romantic associations, some of them linked to the fortunes of the royal families. Most of the clan tartans worn in the nineteenth century were fairly recent inventions, as the early wearers of tartan did not adopt particular setts (patterns) or colours to denote their clans.

The fashion for tartan was fuelled by a keen antiquarian interest in Highland dress during the early nineteenth century. Sir Walter Scott (1771–1832) was instrumental in raising awareness of Scotland's traditions, both through his Waverley novels and the role he played in welcoming King George IV to Edinburgh in 1822. The Royal visit sparked a tartan frenzy, with Scott encouraging the wearing of clan tartans and the King's appearance in a kilt, tartan coat and plaid. The publication of James Logan's *The Scottish Gael* (1831), which recorded fifty-five different setts, and the controversial *Vestiarium Scoticum* (1842) also had a major impact. Many of the patterns were invented but they spurred on manufacturers to produce new clan tartans for clients and the fashion industry.

The tartan on this waistcoat is probably a version of the 'Prince Charles Edward' design that appears in a book of tartan patterns produced by W & A Smith of Mauchline.[1] Although it is similar to Stewart tartans, this particular design did not exist before the 1850s.

1. W & A Smith, *The Authenticated Tartans of the Clans and Families of Scotland* (Mauchline, 1850).

Man's waistcoat of woven silk velvet with a ribbed silk back.
British, about 1850
Given by Mrs E. Alliott
T.133-1967

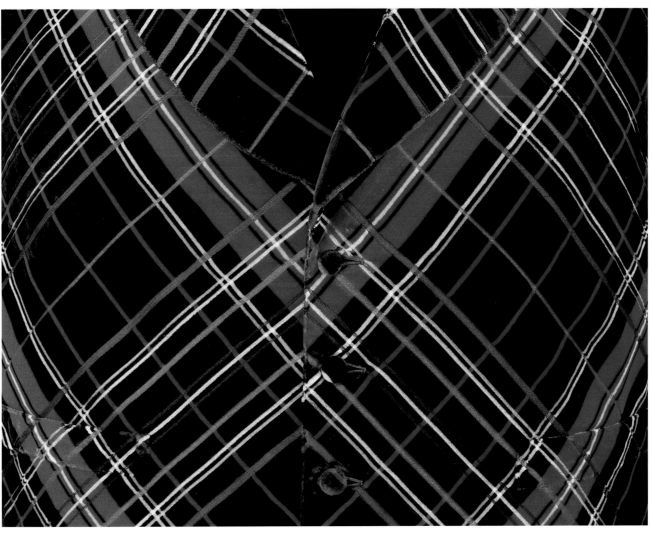

Romantic
Styles

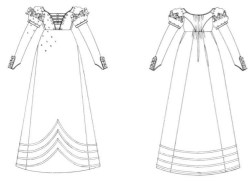

Fancy borders in all manner of designs trimmed the skirts of 1820s evening dresses. Festooned flounces interspersed with roses, puffs of net ornamented with rosettes, embroidered floral sprigs and applied leaf or shell designs threw the hems into three-dimensional relief. Rouleaux, composed of tubular lengths of bias-cut fabric padded out with lambs' wool, were a favourite decorative device. Four satin rouleaux surround the bottom edge

of this gown, rising to a point in the centre front, which complements the trimmings on the bodice and sleeves. Sometimes rouleaux were adorned with ribbons, entwined with pearls or edged with deep falls of lace.

Light silk slips worn beneath these dresses enhanced their diaphanous effects. White, pale blue and pink underdresses were popular, often contrasting with the trimmings or colour of the gown. *The Ladies' Monthly Museum* of 1824 refers to dresses of 'white net over blue satin', 'white *crêpe lisse*, over a pink satin slip' and 'yellow crape over a white satin slip. Border ornamented with three white satin rouleaux.' Evocative names such as 'celestial blue', 'maiden's-blush rose' and 'turquoise blue stone' added to their ethereal quality.

Evening dress of silk gauze embroidered with silk and trimmed with silk satin (the cream silk underdress is a replica).
British, 1820–24
Given by Miss Alice A. Little
T.101-1922

A rope trimming anchors the hem of this skirt so that it falls in graceful folds to the floor. It provides an interesting contrast to the soft dreamy look of the dress woven with delicate bands of coloured threads. Perhaps the wearer wanted to make a statement or it was made by an amateur who lacked the skills to make a wadded hem. The fact that the seams are unfinished also suggests that this gown was made at home rather than by a professional dressmaker. The total effect, however, makes up for any flaws in its construction. In artificial light the slivers of pink, blue and green silk would have shimmered against the gossamer-light gauze like reflections sparkling on water.

Evening dress made of silk gauze woven with silk threads (the cream silk underdress is a replica).
British, 1810–20
Given by Miss Dorothea Williams
T.2-1952

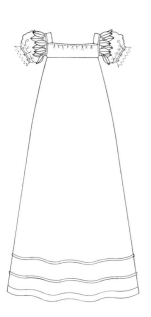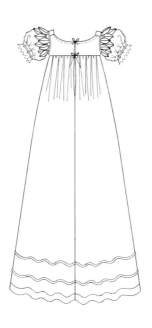

This pink dream of a dress epitomizes romantic styles in fashion. It is made of patterned silk gauze with an all-over design of pink dots and would have been worn over a white or coloured silk satin slip. The earlier vertical simplicity of the neo-classical dress is now broken by a stiffened hem decoration that gives the skirt the desired weight and silhouette of the period. Here, a broad band of pink silk satin edged with rouleaux near the lower hem helps the skirt fall into a soft trapezoid shape.

The puffed sleeves resemble flower cups with their layered pink and gauze petals on a foundation of cream net edged with blonde lace. It fastens at the back of the bodice with drawstrings at the neck and the high waist. The dress has an incredibly short bodice, only five centimetres deep, which could barely have covered the wearer's bosom.
H. P.

Ball dress of patterned white silk gauze with pink dots (the cream silk underdress is a replica).
British, *c*.1815
T.3-1952

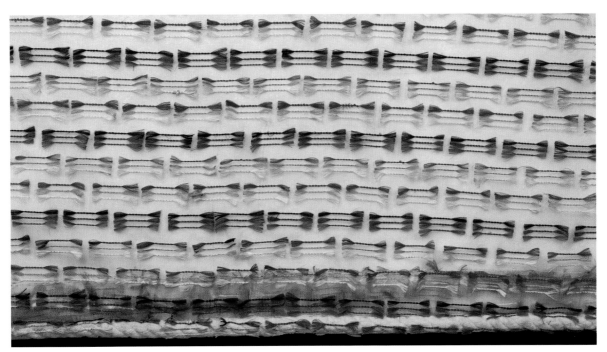

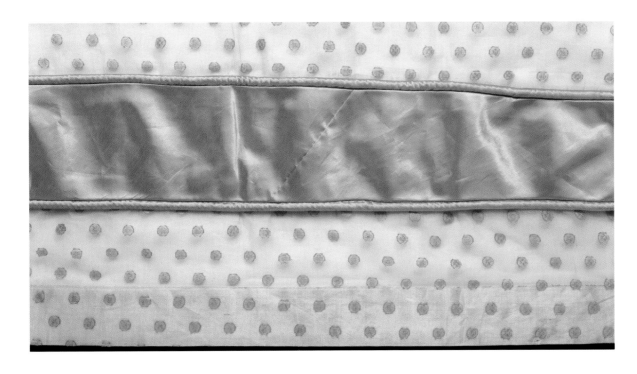

Balloon-like sleeves billow out from the shoulders of this printed cotton day dress. By the 1830s sleeves had reached such exaggerated proportions that women were compared to 'ants' and 'bottle spiders' with their tiny waists and bell-shaped skirts. There were at least a dozen different patterns for sleeves for day wear with romantic names such as 'Cavalier', 'Donna Maria', 'Sultan', 'Medici' and 'Marino Faliéro'. These are examples of 'Gigot' sleeves, which were very full at the shoulder, diminishing in size towards the elbow and becoming tight at the wrist. They are made in two pieces and the fabric is matched on the front seam so that the join is barely visible.

The challenge with sleeves of this size was how to support them as they were often made of flimsy materials. Some styles had stiff buckram undersleeves or hoops to give them their shape. But these are unlined so the wearer probably attached a large down-filled pad to each arm just below the shoulder line over which the sleeves distended. Feathers have the advantage of being easily compressed so that the pad could be squeezed through the narrow armhole of the dress.

Dress made of printed cotton decorated with a metal buckle.
British, 1830–34
Given by Messrs Harrods Ltd
T.168-1915

By the summer of 1836 flamboyant romantic fashions had submitted to a more restrained style in dress. The once exuberant sleeve collapsed, becoming close-fitting in the upper arm to highlight the graceful sloping shoulder line. Focus shifted away from billowing curves to a more angular silhouette inspired by 'Gothic' forms. Gradually bodices became much longer in the waist with a deep point at the centre front and a greater emphasis on the figure.

This dress has 'Bishop' sleeves, which were set low off the shoulder and very full to the wrist where they were gathered into a tight cuff. In this example, the fullness of the upper arm has been drawn into horizontal rows of puffed shirring, formed by a series of parallel running stitches which fix the fabric in between into gathers. 'Bishop' sleeves were usually made of light materials and not lined so that they hung limp to emphasize the fashionable drooping line.

The bodice is typical of late 1830s styles with its low neckline and pointed waist. The distinctive seams are reinforced with decorative piping and fan up from the waist to emphasize the closer-fitting line. It is probable that this dress was remodelled from an earlier garment.

Bodice and skirt made of pink silk trimmed with blonde lace, lined with glazed cotton and whalebone strips.
British, 1838–40
Given by Mrs O. T. Wade
T.257-1968

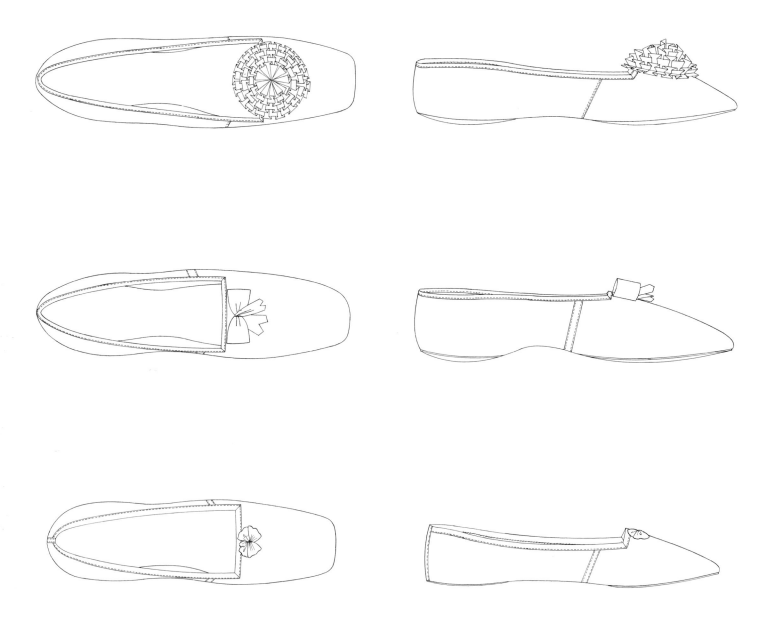

As skirts became wider and shorter, attention focused on the foot and ankle. Brightly coloured silk shoes complemented the richness of 1830s dresses, often matching the sash or long fluttering ribbons worn in the hat. They came in a wide variety of colours, including 'canary yellow', 'palm-leaf green' and 'marshmallow blossom'. Delicate bows and rosettes enhanced the daintiness of the foot. In 1834 *The World of Fashion* reported, 'Some of our fashionables have made exchange in the slipper, lacing it up the front with coloured ribbons … the rosettes are worn larger than they were, and ornaments in various styles will probably be introduced for dress shoes.' Rosettes became increasingly fashionable and the white shoe pictured here has been customized as the rosette has been applied on top of an existing bow. It is made from one piece of ribbon which has been box pleated in concentric circles and then sewn onto a circular buckram backing. The elastic tie just visible on the inner is also a later addition and would have fastened around the ankle to keep the shoe in place.

Due to their fragility, silk 'slippers' were usually reserved for indoor wear, evening dress or special occasions. Looking at these examples it is not difficult to see why. Although the toes are lined with linen and the back of the upper with kid, they were clearly not made to last. Some writers complained that silk shoes became distorted and ugly after a few days' wear. They were also probably uncomfortable as the toes are narrow, square and very shallow.

Women's shoes made of silk satin lined with kid and linen with a flat leather sole.
British, 1830s–40s
Given by: Thomas W. Grieg (top), C. M. Buckley (middle), Messrs Harrods Ltd (bottom)
From top to bottom: 2218-1899, T.178-1962, T.503-1913

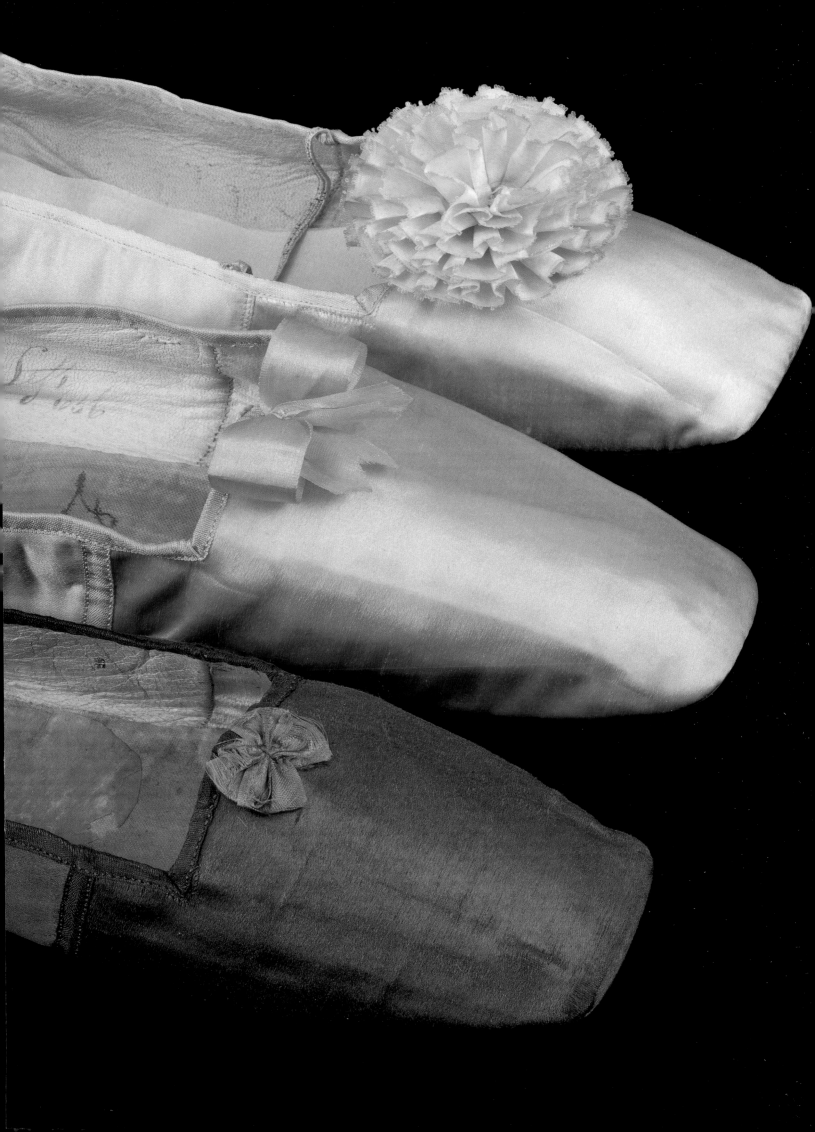

During the 1820s and 1830s, vibrant, imaginative and exuberant styles in women's dress captured a sense of romantic fantasy. Skirts fanned out from tiny waists, enormous sleeves ballooned from the shoulders, ribbons fluttered from lavishly adorned bonnets, and flowers, feathers, jewels and bows bedecked the hair. To add to the effect, elaborate trimmings such as vandyked collars and stomacher-style bodices created a nostalgic reference to the styles of the seventeenth and eighteenth centuries.

White muslin was popular as it emphasized the graceful, billowing forms and provided a blank canvas for decorative detail. Both day and evening dresses were often embroidered around the hem with wreaths of flowers, half-opening roses, interweaving sprigs of foliage and vine leaves. Colours tended to be soft and harmonious, reflecting the dreamy quality of these gowns. Helen, the heroine of Emily Eden's novel *The Semi-Attached Couple*, clearly created a dreamlike impression when she '… came in, looking like a genuine angel, so soft and white and bright'.[1]

1. Emily Eden, *The Semi-Attached Couple* (1860; written about 1830), Ch.XXVIII.

Dress of muslin embroidered with stylized rosebuds and foxgloves. Trimmed with silk satin and wadded rouleaux.
British or French, about 1830
Given by Mr Le Cocq
T.51-1934

The waisted frock coat came into fashion in about 1816 and became an enduring style. It was worn for everyday purposes such as morning dress, usually with a top hat, cane and trousers. Features that characterized the frock coat included a narrow waist and full skirts hanging vertically in front. These gave it certain benefits as the tailor Francis Edwards pointed out: 'For showing off the proportions of the figure, a frock has a great advantage over the dress coat, as there is a cleaner sweep in the skirts of the former which is better calculated to contrast the waist and chest.'[1]

By 1830 frock coats were made in a variety of designs according to taste, fashion or type of activity. This example has an outbreast pocket, a feature which appeared on coats during the 1830s. The graceful crescent-shape is echoed in the two larger pockets located on either side of the skirt fronts. All are bound with velvet to match the collar and lapels, giving cohesion and added elegance to the design.

1. Francis Edwards, *A History of English Dress; or the Fashions Past and Present* (London, 1845), p.62.

Man's double-breasted frock coat of woollen beaver cloth trimmed with silk velvet.
British or French, 1830s
Given by Mr Robert Spence
T.61-1936

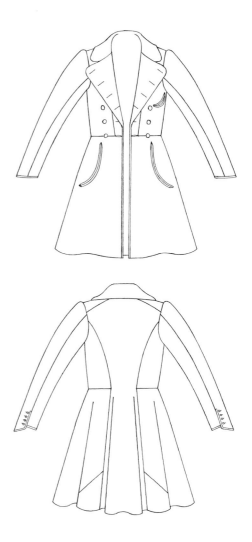

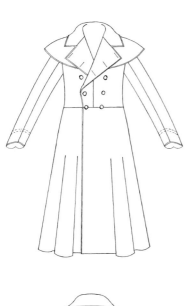

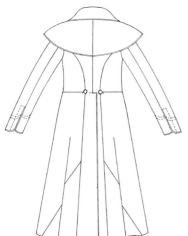

This elegant frock coat epitomizes the romantic style of 1820s men's dress. In line with this fashion, attention is lavished on features to exaggerate the human form such as broad shoulders and a narrow waist. The general silhouette also mirrors women's costume of the period with their expanding sleeves and widening skirts.

In cutting and shaping the garment, the tailor has employed several clever devices to achieve this look. The cape extending under the collar increases the width of the shoulders and the wide lapels accentuate the fullness of the chest. To emphasize the smallness of the waist the coat has been fitted very close to the body at this point. This tight fit could result in an unsightly crease at the waist, so the tailor has introduced a 'waist-seam'. Waist-seams became a popular feature on 1820s frock coats as they helped ensure a smooth line. They originated from a small horizontal dart which was cut to eliminate creasing in the hollow above the hips and was known as 'taking out a fish'.

Man's double-breasted frock coat of superfine with silk velvet collar and needlewoven buttons.
British, 1820s
Given by Mr Talbot Hughes
T.294-1910

Delicate floral sprays and gentle colours give this bodice a soft, feminine appeal. The diaphanous wool gauze woven with a silk stripe enhances the effect. Light materials such as printed gauze and muslin were popular for day and evening wear, and ribbon bows in harmonious colours provided attractive trimmings. The sleeve borders and skirt flounces on this example are printed with a separate pattern so that they complement the shape of the dress. This style of printing and weaving was popular in the late 1850s and 1860s as it emphasized the width of the sleeves and skirt.

The surplus fabric on the front of this bodice has been starched and then gathered into pleats that are caught onto the lining. This focuses attention on the shape of the bodice and accentuates the narrow waist. Three whalebone supports inserted into the lining and spreading up fan-wise from the waist act as a foundation support and help prevent the fabric from wrinkling in unsightly creases. To provide further structure, the dress would have been worn over a corset and crinoline or horsehair petticoat.

Bodice of printed wool gauze woven with a silk stripe and trimmed
with silk fringe and silk chiné ribbon. Lined with cotton and whalebone strips.
British, 1855–60
Given by Mrs Wilkinson
T.145-1970

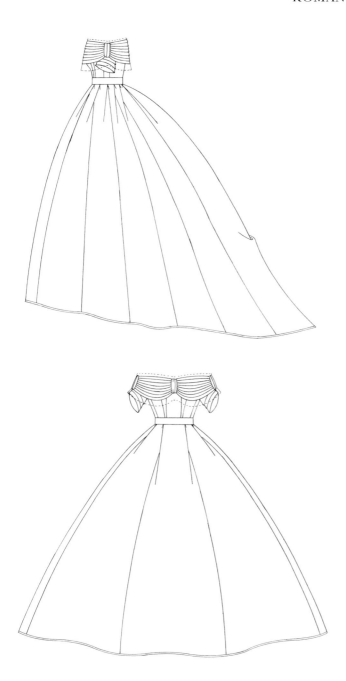

The bride's dress was a focal point of the wedding just as it often is today. Its design can therefore give us an important insight into Victorian custom and social convention. The fashionable cut and rich materials lavished on this gown show that it was clearly designed for a prosperous wedding. With its crisp, simple lines, high waist and gored skirt worn over a crinoline cage, it is similar to styles depicted in contemporary photographs and fashion plates. The shimmering silk satin, delicate lace trimmings and pleated bertha give the dress a sumptuous quality as would have befitted a wealthy bride.

The colour is also significant as brides of social standing tended to wear white, ivory or cream. The fashion for white wedding dresses started in the mid-eighteenth century, although most people were married in coloured gowns. By the early nineteenth century more and more women opted for white as it implied purity, cleanliness and social refinement. The less well off or more practically minded opted for pale blue, dove grey or fawn, which they could wear for special occasions long after the event.

It was, however, acceptable and even desirable for fashionable brides to customize their dresses for the early days of married life. In this example there is evidence that long net sleeves were once attached to the short oversleeves and a chemisette would probably have covered the neck. As weddings took place during the day it was usually considered unseemly to reveal a low décolletage or bare arms. Net was ideal as it provided a modest covering without destroying the effect of the dress and could easily be removed to create a fashionable evening gown.

Wedding dress (bodice and skirt) of silk satin trimmed with needle lace. Bodice lined with cotton and whalebone strips.
USA, about 1865
Given by Mrs Campbell
T.37-1951

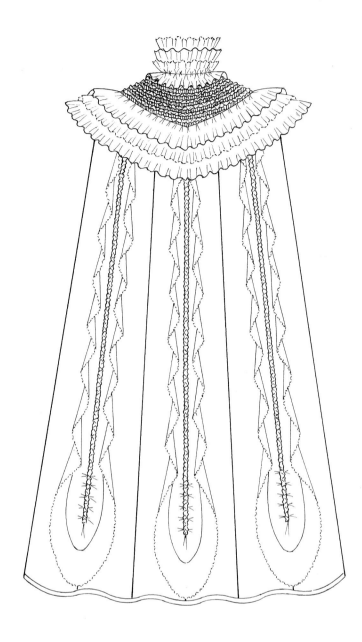

A froth of lace and chiffon cascades from the neck and shoulders of this elegant opera cloak by Worth. The pastel shades and layers of diaphanous fabrics show how fashion was moving towards a softer, dreamier look towards the end of the century. Curved steel supports attached to the lining at the shoulders emphasize the fashionable sweeping silhouette as it falls away into the main body of the gown. The couturier has left the panels of silk satin comparatively unadorned as he wished to focus attention on the face of the wearer. He also intended to highlight the richness of the pattern where feather-like leaves and striking flowers adorn a garden trellis.

By the time this cloak was made, Charles Frederick Worth (1825–95), the founder of Maison Worth, was dead. Yet his legacy remained in the care of his sons, who ensured that the tradition of using only the best materials would endure. House hallmarks of boldly patterned silks, innovative use of fabrics and lavish ornament continued during the decades flanking 1900. Fashionable clients from across the world, from princesses to the nouveau-riches, flocked to be an owner of a Worth confection. Garments like this one were worn over dazzling dresses for visits to the opera, theatre, receptions, state functions and lavish balls.

Woman's opera cloak made of silk satin woven with a self-coloured pattern. Trimmed with chiffon and machine lace.
Jean-Philippe Worth (1856–1926). French, 1897–1900
T.86-1991

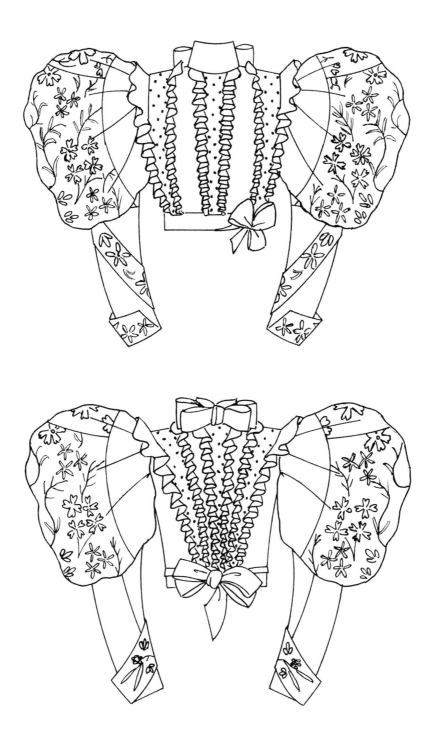

Enormous sleeves swell out from the bodice of this 1890s day dress, creating an exaggerated shoulder line and emphasizing the smallness of the waist. They were known as 'gigot' sleeves and were highly fashionable between 1894 and 1896 when women adopted them for all types of activities and occasions. The basic shape was similar to that of the 1830s, and like those sleeves they rapidly diminished in size after a few years.

The upper portion of this sleeve is constructed in four parts and is attached to a lower sleeve that is tight to the wrist. It is also mounted onto a foundation sleeve that helps support the puffed section, which is typical for sleeves of this date. Many were full of praise for their extravagant shape and *Le Moniteur de la Mode, The Ladies Magazine* of August 1894 commented: 'The new gigot is one of the handsomest, most stylish sleeves which can be made. Full and draped above the elbow, yet tight below.'

Bodice made of silk satin decorated with raised embroidery and trimmed with sequinned net. Lined with silk and whalebone strips.
Mml. L. Guiquin, Robes et Manteaux. New York, 1895
Given by Major and Mrs Broughton
T.271-1972

Etiquette dictated that a woman of society vary her costume according to the time of day. She also needed several different types of evening dress to suit different occasions, although a lady reserved her most decorative gowns for the ballroom, where the luxurious fabrics, lavish trimmings and sparkling jewels could be displayed to breathtaking effect. May Littledale (née Primrose) wore this romantic ball dress shortly after her marriage to Henry Littledale in 1885.

The gown is at the height of fashion for its time. The heavily-boned bodice is laced behind like a corset and extends into a deep point, which gracefully curves over the back of the skirt. This emphasizes the tiny waist and bustled silhouette that were hallmarks of stylish dress in the mid-1880s. The bodice is also cut fairly high on the hips to allow for the folds of moiré draped across the front and sides of the dress to complement the huge

bow. During this period drapery was often composed of separate pieces mounted onto the foundation skirt, rather than being formed by the cut of the skirt. A small cushion sewn into the back of the waist and a stiffened lining pulled into shape by tapes help the skirt project behind while remaining flat in front.

The shimmering silk seems to float on the machine-lace over-skirt creating light and airy effects well suited to the ballroom. Lace was a popular trimming for evening dress and *Myra's Home Journal* of February 1885 extolled its virtues: 'Lace is very much used, and the skirt then becomes a mere foundation, showing off the rich pattern of the lace tunic or flounces. It is not, however, necessary that the flounces should be of real lace; imitation laces are now so well made, and in such handsome patterns, that they are used in the same way.'

Ball gown (bodice and skirt) of silk overlaid and trimmed with machine lace. Bodice lined with silk, cotton and whalebone strips.
British, about 1885
Given by the Hon. Mrs Tyser in memory of the Dowager Lady Remnant
T.429-1990

Exoticism

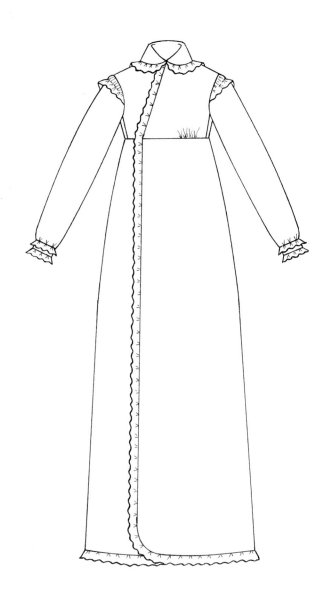

The fabric used in this stylish wrap-over gown is an unusual example of Indian ikat, purposely made to attract the European market. Ikat is a Malay term for a complex tie-resist dyeing technique in which the warp (or the weft) threads are dyed to form the pattern before weaving. The soft and blurred transition between the different coloured parts of the pattern is created by the displacement of the threads while weaving.

The wrap-over gown with round, slightly raised collar is adorned with gathered trimmings and narrow shoulder frills. It has excessively long sleeves which would have been bunched up decoratively around the wrists when the wristbands were fastened. The bodice is only lined at the back panel with white cotton, and the excess of the skirt is gathered at the back. Originally there would have been fastening bands at the waist, but these are now missing. At some point the length of the skirt was adjusted with a tuck around the hem.

H. P.

Peignoir of ikat muslin.
British, of Indian fabric, *c*.1812–14
Given by Messrs Harrods Ltd
T.798-1913

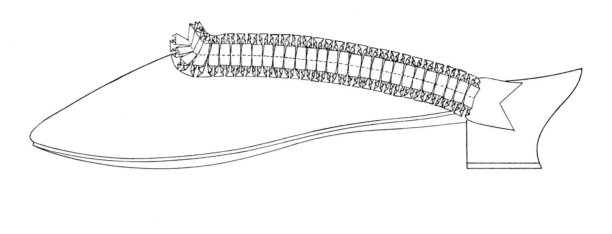

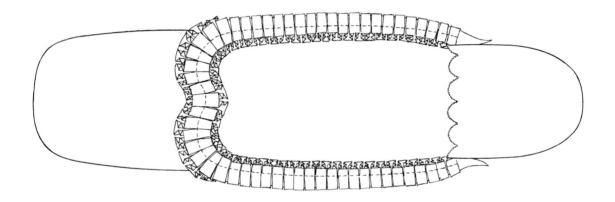

A stylized tulip flanked by two rosebuds decorates the toe of this elegant shoe. The buds seem about to burst into bloom, elegantly framing the central flower. Mules (backless shoes) became fashionable for indoor wear during the 1850s and were made in a variety of colours and designs. Some were quilted or lined with fur, others woven with elaborate designs or embroidered with beads. Middle Eastern motifs were popular and the fabric for the upper on this example has been tapestry-woven in Turkey then exported to Europe to be made up into a shoe.

The shoemaker has skilfully positioned the design so that the main tulip lies at the centre of the toe, and a silk trimming has been selected to complement the colour of the flowers. It is made from a single piece of ribbon which has been stitched into double box pleats creating a ruched effect. The heel is covered in red leather to match the trimming. Heeled shoes like this one were often made as 'straights', which meant that they were not shaped to the left and right foot. Technological progress meant that footwear could be cut in lefts and rights, but many women continued to wear straights until about 1900.

Woman's mule, tapestry-woven with a floral design and trimmed with silk ribbon.
Fabric woven in Turkey, shoe made up in Britain or France, 1870s
Bequeathed by A. F. Kendrick
Circ.553-1954

Richly embroidered white satin studded with turquoise glass and metal gives this gown an opulent feel. During the 1890s, couturiers often embellished their evening wear with a profusion of embroidery in undulating vegetal curves and floral swirls. Such designs gave rise to the belief that jewels adorned garments, although in reality most of them were not made of precious stones.

The metallic embroidery on this example was probably executed in North India for the European market and therefore presents a hybrid design largely dictated by Western tastes. Embroidery using metal thread was known by the generic term *zardozi* (gold embroidery), and flourished during the nineteenth century when a wide range of techniques was employed. Here, purls (cords of twisted metal thread) are used in a variety of ways, some worked in loops to define the outline of the foliage; others laid over a foundation padding of cotton threads to throw the petals and leaves into relief.

Cascades of lace, richly patterned silk and turquoise satin

heighten the lavish appeal of this tea-gown and complement the colour and design of the embroidery. Although tea-gowns were originally designed in the 1870s as easy, comfortable garments appropriate for taking five o'clock tea, they soon became increasingly elaborate and fitted. By the 1890s luxurious confections combining exotic fabrics, historical influences and fantasy were worn for more public appearances such as dinner parties. One component they still shared with earlier designs was the distinctive Watteau pleat which fell from the centre back of the neckline to the floor, resembling sack-back gowns of the eighteenth century.

The Queen of September 1900 describes a tea-gown very similar to the one pictured here and suggests the impact it could have on the beholder: 'The lace falls in soft Watteau drapery at the back, the sleeves, which fall over the hand, are of lace, and the pieces at the sides are lined with a kilting of chiffon. It is quite a perfect gown, showing soft falling kilted flounces at the hem, silk muslin or silk serving to enhance the beauty of incomparable lace.'

Tea-gown of woven damask embroidered with glass, metal beads and purl. Decorated with chain-stitch embroidered net.
Plastron panel probably embroidered in North India, possibly Delhi, for the French market.
Lace made in Limerick, Ireland. Gown designed by Rouff. France, about 1900
T.87-1991

This bustle pad is made of 'paisley-style' printed fabric with a bright red ground and yellow, blue, black and white details. The distinctive pattern is largely based on designs for Indian woven shawls from Kashmir. Western designers adapted the traditional 'buta'[1] or 'pine' motifs for more cheaply produced printed cottons used in making petticoats, handkerchiefs and scarf borders. Colourful and elaborate patterns also evolved which were highly stylized to accommodate fashionable tastes of the day.

The bustle pad is lined with red cotton on the underside and has a faint printed maker's label in black from which can be discerned 'Leech Arctic Down'. There is evidence of two pairs of tapes, one at the waist and the other on the hips, for securing the pad. Designed to be worn over petticoats, this lightweight pad would give lift and buoyancy to the voluminous bustles of the 1870s. The down filling would be most likely goose or duck down imported from Canada.

M. K.

1. Flower or bush.

Bustle pad made of printed cotton filled with feathers.
'Leech Arctic Down'. British, about 1870
Given by the executors of the late Mr E. W. Mynott
T.69-1980

The elaborate design filling the front edge of this dolman is typical of the kind woven onto shawls in India for the European market. Kashmir shawls had been fashionable in Europe since the late eighteenth century and reached the peak of their popularity during the 1850s and 1860s when they were worn over crinoline skirts. By then French and British agents dominated the Kashmir shawl industry and they brought more patterns from Europe for local weavers to copy. As a result, designs became increasingly overblown, often combining genuine Indian motifs with European influences and new colours.

Political and economic forces led to a decline in the demand for exported shawls during the 1870s. The style of dress was also changing and the advent of the slimmer silhouette and bustled skirt meant that shawls became unwieldy and unnecessary additions to the woman's wardrobe. However they were still sometimes given as wedding gifts or transformed into figure-hugging mantles lavishly trimmed and lined to match the colours of the shawl pattern.

For more information on this dolman see page 184.

Woman's dolman of woven wool lined with quilted silk satin and trimmed with a twisted silk and chenille fringe.
Woven in India for the European market, 1878–82
Given by T. R. H. The Duke and Duchess of Gloucester
T.44-1957

Fern-like fronds and stylized carnations meander across the bottom edge of this man's cloak. The overall pattern depicts numerous leaves, flowers and curving stems in a fantastical arrangement of form, balanced and restrained by a precisely defined border. Each motif is hand-embroidered to form the outline and fill in the details, while the woollen cloth provides a dark ground highlighting the intensity of colour.

This design was embroidered in Kashmir for the European market and is very similar to patterns commonly seen on exported shawls. Needleworkers (*rafugars*) had traditionally been employed in the shawl-weaving process to repair and join together the individual pieces that made up the garment. During the early nineteenth century they began to embroider the entire shawl, copying the woven originals as well as following new patterns. This was introduced as a cost-cutting measure as embroidered shawls were easier and quicker to manufacture.

The lining and position of the borders down the front and along the hem of the cloak imitate those on Indian *choghas* (loose coats). In terms of construction, however, the cloak copies European fashions with its stiffened collar and cape.

Man's cloak of superfine embroidered with coloured silk threads and part-lined with silk.
Embroidered in Kashmir for the European market, 1850s
Given by K. Baker
T.75-1964

This feather-filled padded petticoat of printed cotton is constructed from five 'A'-shaped panels machine-sewn together, lined with a plain red cotton then stitched to form eight tubular sections from hem to hip. The top section is left unfilled and pleated into a waistband, but each of the eight tubular sections is filled with feathers and down for padding. A label in the waistband reads:

BOOTH & FOX
ARCTIC GOOSE DOWN SKIRTS
36". Fast colours. Wash with down in. Shake when drying

Indian influences can clearly be seen in the tear-drop 'buta'[1] motifs which are printed on a red ground in colours of blue, green, yellow and black. The bright red dye is based on madder and became known as Turkey or Adrianople red. It was popular, and the development of production modifications in the nineteenth century made it readily affordable. Goose down was also plentiful and inexpensive. The petticoat was colourful, warm, lightweight and washable.

M. K.

1. Flower or bush.

Petticoat of printed cotton filled with goose down.
Booth & Fox. British, about 1860
Gift of Mrs I. Gadsby-Toni
T.212-1962

Delicate floral sprays and twisted woody stems trail across this fashionable day dress. The pattern is interspersed with teardrop shapes known as buta[1] motifs, which are based on Indian designs. India occupied a special place in British life throughout the nineteenth century, and textile manufacturers adopted traditional Indian patterns enthusiastically for dress and furnishing fabrics. This particular design is derived from border and field patterns on woven Kashmir shawls, which had a strong influence on printed fabrics during this period. The fusion of buta motifs and quasi-naturalistic floral forms reflects the passion for blending exotic influences with European embellishments.

Bright colours on a dark ground were popular during the 1830s and were achieved through a combination of printing techniques. The brown fancy machine-ground in this example has been printed using an engraved metal cylinder to achieve the mottled effect. This process, known as cylinder or roller-printing, was introduced in the late eighteenth century and proved much quicker than block-printing by hand, thereby reducing labour costs. By the 1830s it had become a highly mechanized technique, although it was still difficult to print more than two or three colours simultaneously. Extra colours were therefore often added by hand-block printing or by using wooden surface rollers, cut in the same way as wood blocks.

1. Flower or bush.

Dress of printed cotton lined with cotton.
British, 1838–40
Given by Mrs C. Rose
T.75-1947

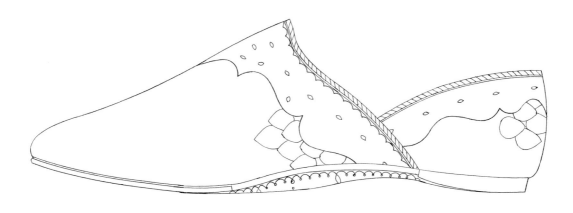

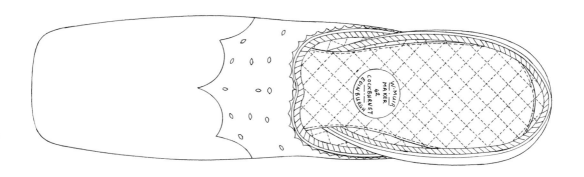

Typical of the period when there was a fascination and demand for exotic animal products for both men and women, this man's slipper is made from the skin of the golden or olive sea snake (*Aipysurus laevis*). This species of sea snake is native to the Northern Territories of Australia, Western Australia, Queensland, The Great Barrier Reef, the Coral Sea, the coasts of New Guinea and Indonesia and would have been imported in large numbers for the production of small items of high-quality leather goods and trimmings. A snake of some two metres in length with large imbricate but somewhat projecting scales, it provides a highly decorative and naturally textured leather ideal for use in making luxury items such as these slippers. The dark, plain leather trim, neatly scalloped, sets off the scale pattern perfectly. The golden silk lining quilted in a diamond pattern, to the size to roughly mimic the scale pattern of the golden sea snake, finishes the slippers with consummate style and panache.
M. K.

Snakeskin slippers with quilted silk lining.
W. Muir, 42 Cockburn Street, Edinburgh. Scottish, 1850s–60s
AP.6-1868

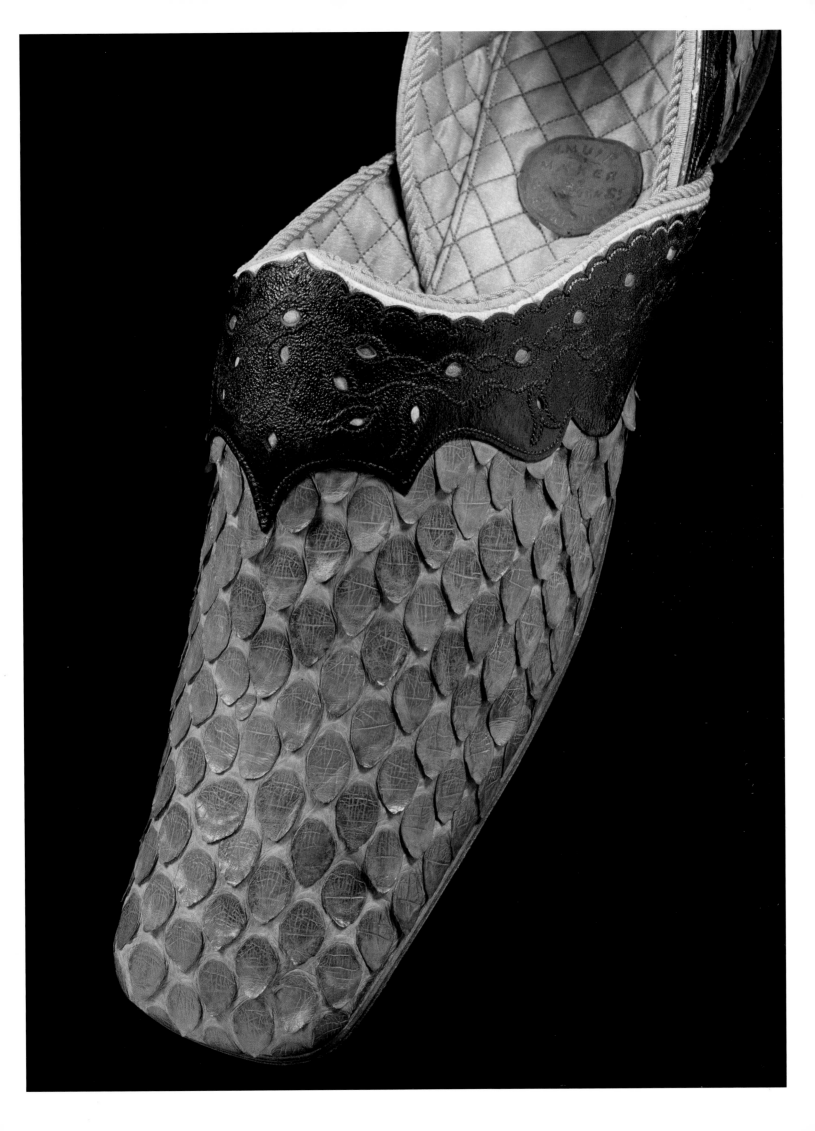

A stuffed hummingbird perching on artificial flowers dominates this Brazilian circular fan or handscreen. It is composed of an ivory handle, base of pink feathers and centre of fluffy white marabou down. Naturally, the hummingbird steals all the attention, but the spray of roses and leaves are so skilfully crafted that only close examination reveals they are made of pink, white and green feathers. The stems are of wire wrapped with silk. Resting on the foliage are three real beetles, iridescent and emerald-like. Fans such as the one shown here were called feather flowers by the manufacturer, and would enhance the fashions for balls, soirées, theatres and weddings.

During the last three decades of the nineteenth century there was a passion for using parts of dead animals as ornaments, both for the person and the home. The more exotic the natural history specimen the better. This craze intensified during the 1880s, and in spite of numerous contemporary articles exposing the barbarities inherent in this trade, the fashion persisted. One dealer in London, for instance, claimed to have received 32,000 dead hummingbirds in one delivery, among other birds and birds' parts.
H. P.

Fan of feathers with stuffed hummingbird.
Melles M. and E. Natté. Brazilian, 1880s
Given by Miss Margaret S. Perkin
T.15-1950

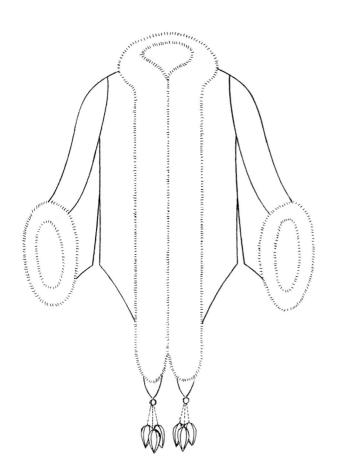 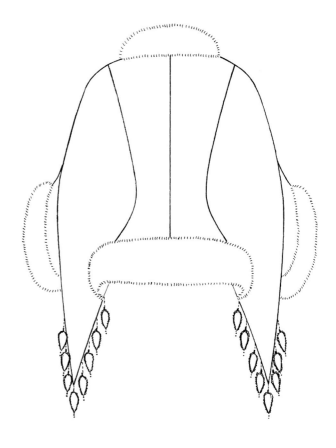

Dolmans were outdoor garments designed to be worn over the fashionable bustles of the 1870s and 1880s. This one is designed so the back would sit comfortably over even the most extreme bustle shape of about 1885. The front, back and sleeves are trimmed with exotic marabou feathers made into wide bands interspersed with small, flat feathers, probably from some type of domestic fowl, and dyed to a lighter tone. This gives an interesting almost sparkle to the trimming as the flat feathers catch the light. Heavy wooden braid-covered pendant tassels are used to trim the pointed panels of the garment. The weight of these provides a contrast to the lightness of the feather decoration and would help keep the hang of the panels, to which they were applied, straight when the dolman was being worn.

Peacocks had been kept in England since Norman times: for decoration in parks and estates, for food, and for the feathers to be used for personal adornment. The feathers had also been used as design elements for woven silks and printed textiles and on many other decorative objects and were particularly popular from the 1860s to 1880s. Marabou trimming, obtained from the downy underwing feathers of the Marabou stork (*Leptoptilos crumeniferus*), became particularly fashionable in the second half of the nineteenth century. These birds were a native species of most parts of the southern two-thirds of Africa. Their downy feathers could be dyed to any colour required and fashioned into long ropes of luxurious trimming, almost fur-like in appearance, as illustrated on this garment. When teamed with rich fabrics and heavy passementerie as here, the effect was stunning.

M. K.

Dolman of cut and uncut velvet with feather trim and braided pendants for decoration.
Redmayne and Co. London, about 1885
Given by Ella Annesley Voysey
T.653-1996

Black and green cock feathers fashion this dramatic cape of the 1890s. It is elbow length with a square cut back and waist-length lappets down the front. Bunches of feathers are mounted onto cotton fabric and lined with black silk satin. The arrangement of the feathers is particularly interesting. Artificially curled feathers cover the bodice and lappets, while larger feathers edge the entire cape. They are denser at the shoulders giving a wing-like effect.

The cape would have been worn over large leg of mutton sleeves which were popular in the mid-1890s. These would have further reinforced the winged shoulder of the cape. The general effect of such an outfit, worn with high heels, would have cut quite an imposing figure. It also graphically captures the sharp comment by one bird activist of the period: 'the feathered woman is a cruel woman'.[1]

H. P.

1. *The Times*, 17 October 1893.

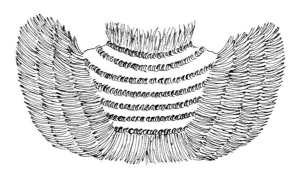

Cape of cock's feathers.
Auguste Champot, 18 Rue de la Michodière, Paris.
French, *c*.1895
Given by Mrs Mailin
T.84-1968

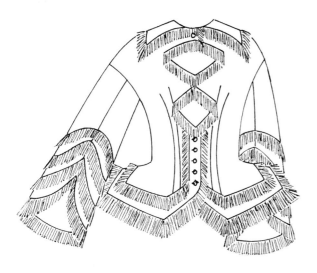

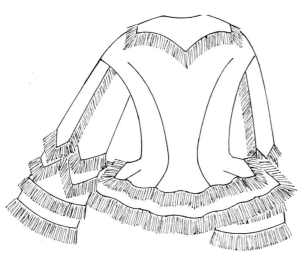

An emerald green jacket bodice flares out behind like the plumage of some exotic bird. This feathery look is achieved through a clever combination of soft texture, colours and layered effects, producing a highly fashionable outfit, perfect for a spring or autumn promenade. Velvet was very popular for outdoor costume, and silk plush, with its long, soft nap, added to the luxurious quality, resembling fine down or sleek fur. Brilliant colours such as green and violet were also much in favour, and trimmings tended to tone in with the colour of the dress rather than contrast with it. Here, the rich fringe is composed of hundreds of strands of crimped silk which would have followed the movements of the wearer and created shimmering illusions in the light. Real fur and feathers were often used as well as simulated effects, and contemporary fashion magazines are full of references to dresses and cloaks embellished with such trimmings.

For more information about this garment see page 180.

Promenade jacket bodice (back view) made of silk plush and trimmed with silk fringe headed with braid. Lined with silk and whalebone strips.
British, 1855–57
Given by Mme Tussauds
T.324-1977

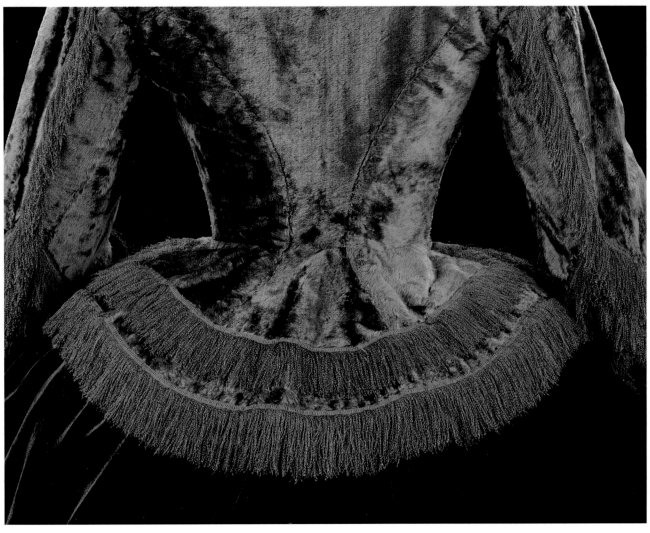

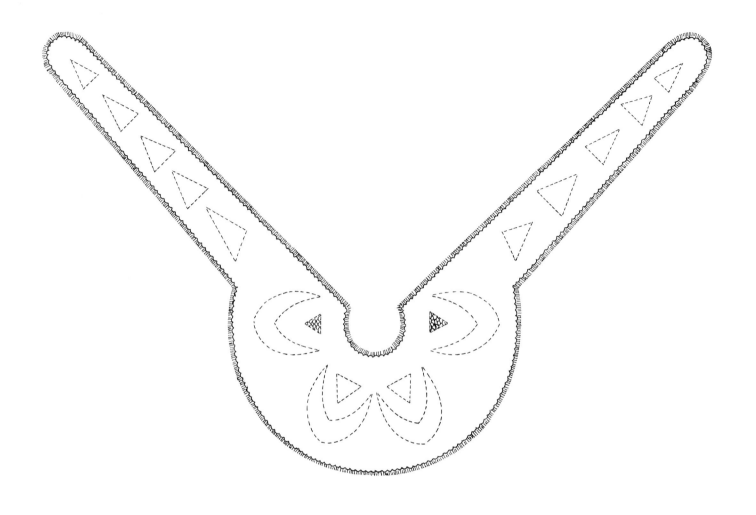

Feathers have been used in clothing of all cultures, as decorative elements or status symbols, but also for warmth and protection. This eye-catching feathered pelerine with long vertical panels at the front was without doubt worn for adornment, while keeping the wearer warm. The clever use of feathers gives the pelerine an unusual and exotic air, although quite a few survive in museum collections and all the birds could be found in England at that time.

Iridescent green and blue peacock feathers make up the vibrant pattern of triangles and half-moons. They contrast dramatically with the surrounding feathers from a range of domestic fowl, dotted and striped in shades of brown and white. Each feather has been attached by hand to cotton buckram, which in turn is lined with a softer cotton fabric covered by tufts of white down. The edge of this cotton fabric has been turned back to make a smooth border. It reveals an unexpectedly coarse stitching, but the pelerine was not supposed to be closely scrutinized for its needlework. There are no remains of any fastening device, but the garment is quite stiff and would have rested securely over a lady's shoulders.

H. P.

Pelerine of peacock and fowl feathers.
British, 1830s
Given by Mrs Shaw
T.28-1910

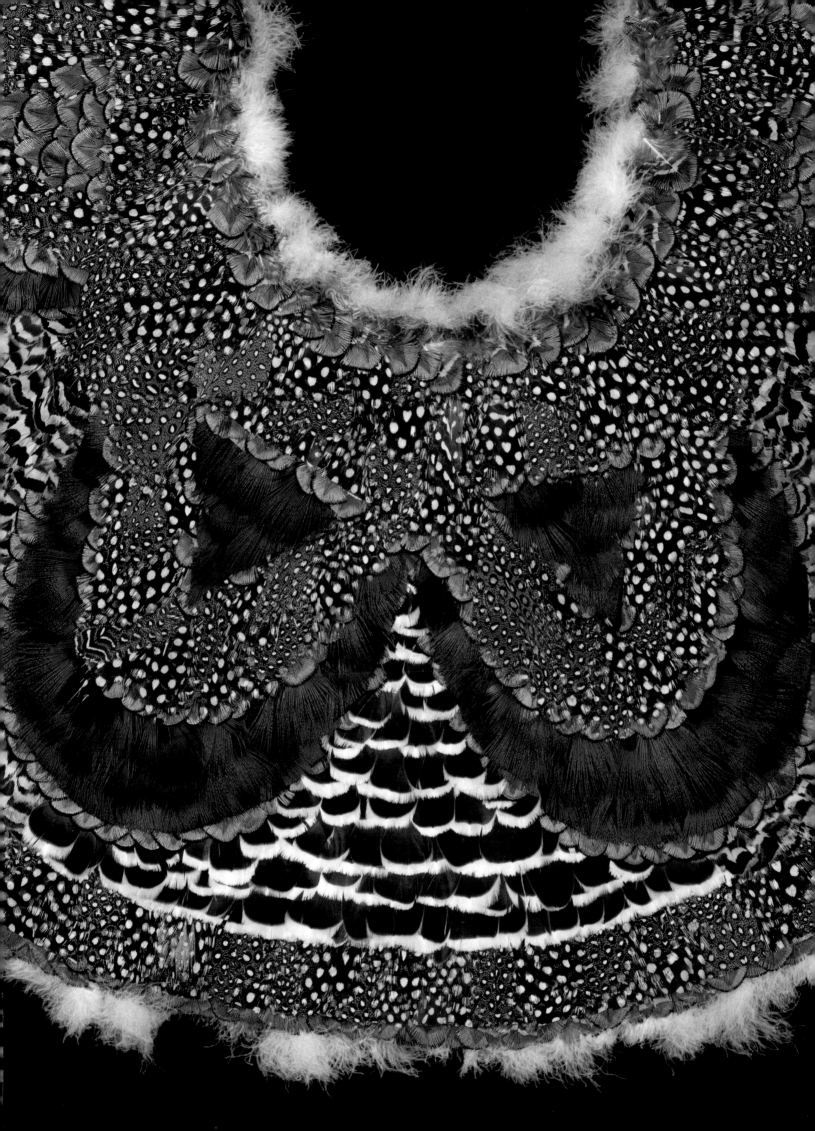

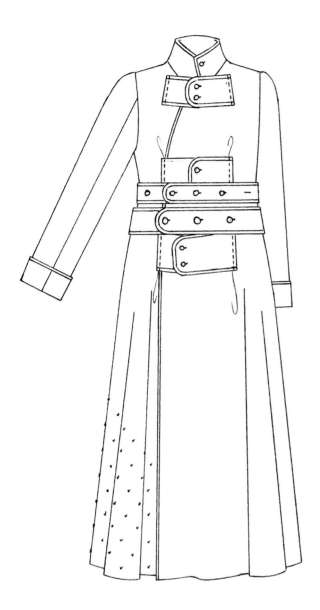
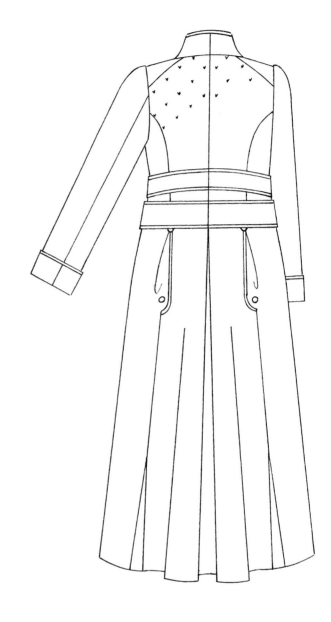

This bizarre flannel dressing gown is decorated with small black woollen tufts in imitation of powdered ermine. Ermine (stoat) (*Mustela erminea*) and squirrel (*Sciurus vulgaris*) were the most popular furs of the late eighteenth and early nineteenth centuries, although many other furs were also worn. Ermine was one of the costliest furs at that time and was fashionable wear for both men and women.

This stylish dressing gown has elaborate fastenings. It was not a unique item as it is one of three similar dressing gowns in a col-lection of clothes worn by Thomas Coutts (1735–1822), who was a partner in the London bank 'Thomas Coutts and Co.'. The dressing gown dates from the latter years of Mr Coutts' life when he was an elderly gentleman, and perhaps the overall style of the garment reflects this, being a little out of date by 1820. However, the garment is of high quality, as befitting a gentleman. It is made from a good-quality fabric and is beautifully constructed and sewn. M. K.

Man's dressing gown of flannel, imitating ermine.
Worn by Thomas Coutts. English, 1815–22
Given by Mr Francis Coutts
Circ.718-1912

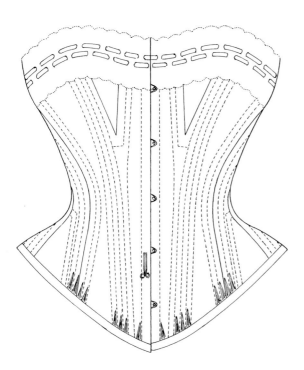
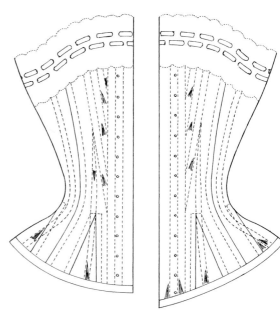

Fuschia pink might seem an exotic choice for Victorian under-wear, but this focus on colour and lavish materials shows the growth in the luxury market for corsetry. Colourful satin corsets became fashionable in the 1880s, challenging the more muted tones of earlier years. Although white and black were still favoured for their practical qualities, pink, 'apricot', red, 'pea-cock-blue' and green with contrasting trimmings were popular. Some models were made of fancy broché, others embroidered with delicate trailing stems, flowers and ears of wheat. Here, the lavishly applied black bobbin lace, threaded with bright pink silk ribbon, adds to the luxurious effect. It draws attention to the

corset and its curvaceous contours, swelling out over the bust and hips. Although it was not meant to be seen, except in private, the attention to detail shows the importance placed on corsetry in a woman's wardrobe. Corset manufacturers capitalized on this, each promising the perfect model in design and decoration as well as comfort and fit. Names such as 'Glove-Fitting', 'Princess', 'Cleopatra' and 'Perfection', as well as trade cards featuring cupids and angels, promoted the corset as a symbol of beauty and femininity.

For more information on this corset see page 144.

Corset of pink satin trimmed with hand-made bobbin lace.
Machine-sewn with hand-flossing and metal slot-and-stud fastening.
British, 1890s
T.738-1974

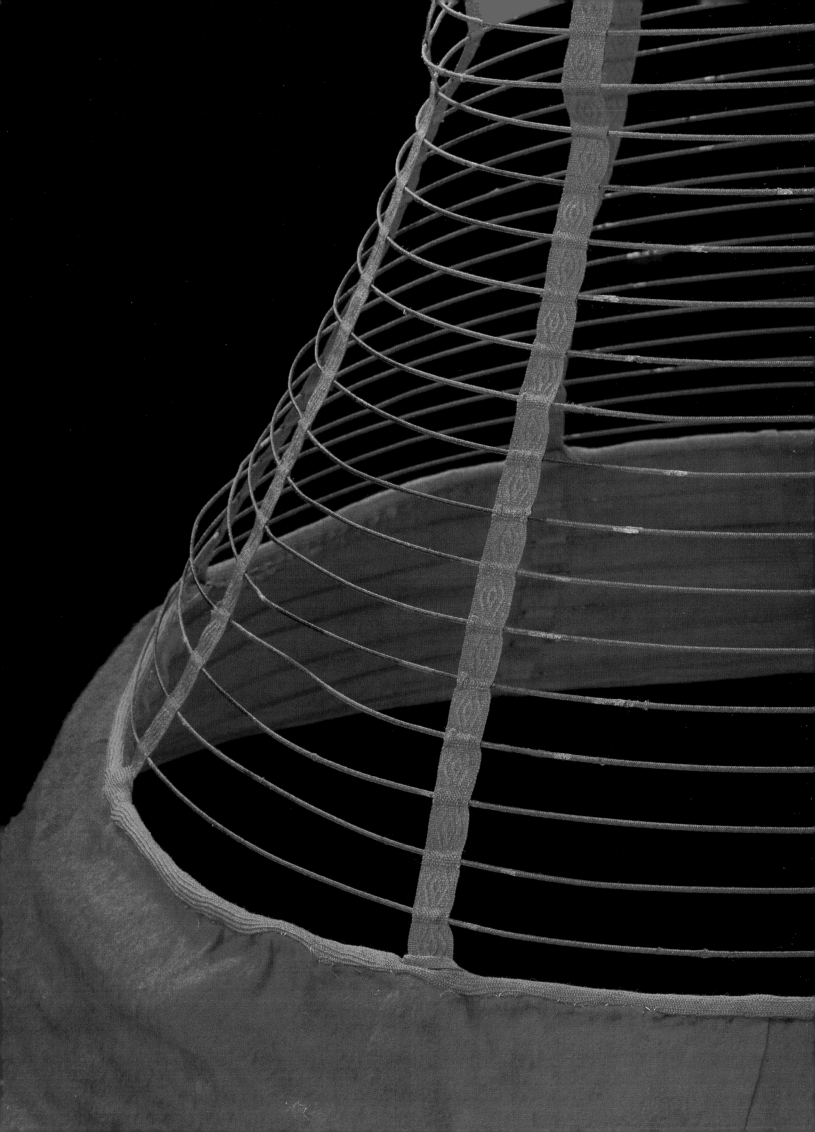

Innovations

A voluminous skirt billows out from the fitted bodice, creating an expanse of intense blue punctuated by woven stripes. Both natural and synthetic dyes were used to generate the dazzling hues that became particularly fashionable in Britain during the 1850s and 1860s, and the streets and drawing rooms must have been awash with colour. Bright blue was a popular colour, and silk a stylish choice for dress fabric as it took the dye very well, producing an intense, glossy sheen. The construction of the skirt acts as a perfect advertisement for the dye as it is thrown out behind by a wide, straight-cut piece of fabric attached to triangular-shaped panels known as gores. Gores were reintroduced in about 1860 so that dresses would hang well over the new style of crinoline frame that was flatter in front and fuller at the back, producing a vast cone-like silhouette.

Not everyone approved of these striking shades, and the French historian Hippolyte Taine (1828–93) found women's dress 'loud and overcharged with ornament' when he visited England in the 1860s. He thought the colours were 'outrageously crude … each swearing at the others' and cited 'violet dresses, of a really ferocious violet'; 'purple or poppy-red silks, grass-green dresses' and 'azure blue scarves' as particularly offensive to the eye. He concluded that 'there can be no doubt that there is something peculiar in the condition of the English retina'.[1]

Isobella Bowhill (1840–1920), the donor's grandmother, is said to have worn this dress to the International Exhibition of 1862 in London. Like many other visitors she may have been impressed by the large case in the middle of the hall labelled 'William Perkin and Sons', containing a solid pillar of mauve dye. The block was said to contain enough colour to dye the heavens purple and was the result of Perkin's discovery of 'aniline violet' in 1856, which led to a revolution in the synthetic dye industry.

1. Hippolyte Taine, *Notes on England 1860–70* (London, 1970), pp19–20, 46, 57, 263–4.

Day dress (bodice and skirt) made of silk, jacquard-woven with a ribbon stripe and trimmed with silk passementerie. Lined with silk, cotton and whalebone strips. Machine-sewn and hand-finished.
British, about 1862
Given by Miss I. Bowhill McClure
T.2-1984

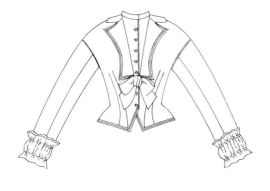

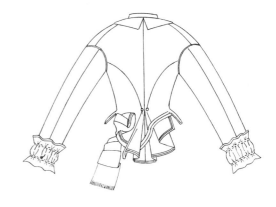

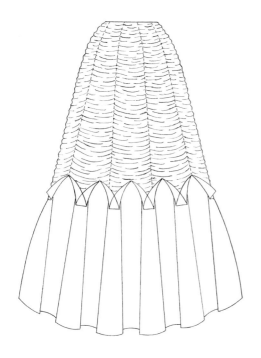

The ruched skirt and draperies on this dress reverberate with intense colour, revealing the fashion for bright new synthetic dyes. Their inception owes much to the work of Sir William Henry Perkin (1838–1907), who discovered the first famous artificial colour by accident in 1856 when he was a student at the Royal College of Chemistry in London. While experimenting with a synthetic formula to replace the natural anti-malarial drug quinine, he produced a reddish powder instead of the colourless quinine. To better understand the reaction he tested the procedure using aniline and created a crude black product that 'when purified, dried and digested with spirits of wine gave the mauve dye'.[1] This dye created a beautiful and lustrous colour that Perkin patented and which became known as 'aniline violet' or 'mauveine'.

Perkin's discovery led to a revolution in synthetic colour from the late 1850s onwards. Textile manufacturers soon turned to his aniline process and the resulting fabrics were characterized by an unprecedented brilliance and intensity that delighted the consumer. Women's dresses acted as a perfect advertisement for these rich hues, especially as the trimmings usually matched the colour of the gown. In August 1859 *Punch* described the craze for purple as 'Mauve Measles', a disease which erupted in 'a measly rash of ribbons' and ended with the entire body covered in mauve. Soon other synthetic dyes were being produced with evocative names such as 'acid magenta', 'aldehyde green', 'Verguin's fuchsine', 'Martius yellow' and 'Magdela red' to match their gaudy appearance. The dress illustrated in this example is coloured with a chemical dye which closely resembles the aniline violet and purple fabric samples dyed with Perkin & Sons Colors shown in the *Practical Mechanics Journal: Record of the Great Exhibition*, 1862.

1. Simon Garfield, *Mauve* (London, 2000), p.36.

Dress (bodice and skirt) of ribbed silk fastened with buttons needlewoven
in silk over a wooden mould. Bodice lined with silk and whalebone strips.
British or French, about 1873
Given by the Marchioness of Bristol, Ickworth, Bury St Edmunds
T.51-1922

Vivid magenta-coloured silk gives this dress a rich and flamboyant appearance. It was probably dyed with one of the new synthetic colours produced from the late 1850s onwards, although intense hues could also be created using natural dyes. The artificial forms of magenta were very popular and a battle for patents began as dyers sought to distinguish their inventions from those of their competitors. In reality many of the dye samples from different manufacturers looked exactly the same, and it was only the exotic names, claims on colourfastness and improved visual quality that set them apart. Other disputes arose over the health risk posed by the wearing and production of garments coloured with synthetic dyes. In the early 1870s a German chemist found traces of arsenic in fabric dyed with magenta, which could leak out in washing, rain or perspiration. There were also reports of serious skin conditions caused by exposure to aniline dyes, and a dye firm in Switzerland was forced to close in 1864 due to arsenic pollution.

Brightly coloured fabrics also led to words of advice from the fashion magazines. *The Englishwoman's Domestic Magazine* of March 1868 recommended that there should be no more than 'two positive colours in a lady's toilet' and that 'very bright tints' should be toned down with white, black or grey to prevent a gaudy appearance. Two shades of the same colour were considered very fashionable, particularly if the trimmings were of a contrasting fabric.[1] In this example, satin bows and pleated bias-cut trimmings complement the ribbed silk perfectly, while delicate puffs of tulle inserted into the sleeves soften the impact of the dramatic colour. These details reveal the skill of eminent couturiers such as Madame Vignon, the maker of this gown, who was also patronized by the fashionable Empress Eugénie, wife of Napoleon III.

1. The difference in colour between the thread and material (see jacket cover) may have become more evident over time.

Dress made with two different bodices, skirt, peplum and bow made
of ribbed silk trimmed with satin. Bodices lined with silk and whalebone strips.
Madame Vignon. Paris, 1869–70
T.118-1979

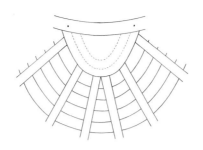

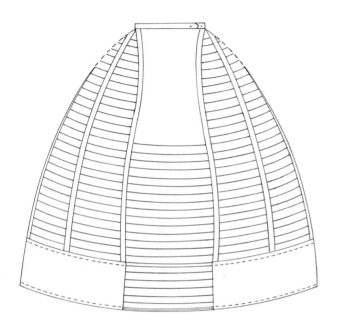

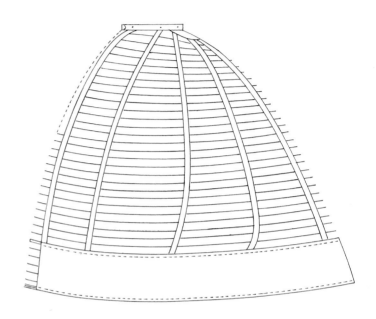

A framework of flexible spring-steel hoops connected by vertical woollen tapes gives this crinoline its distinctive cage-like shape. The word 'crinoline' originally denoted a fabric woven with horsehair that was used as a lining for hats and later to stiffen petticoats and dress hems. By 1856 the term had come to mean a foundation garment composed of graduated steel or whalebone hoops that distended skirts and preserved their shape.

The need for a strong skirt support was very real by the late 1840s. Fashionable skirts had become so full that women had to wear layers of normal and stiffened petticoats underneath to give them any semblance of the desired silhouette. This was uncomfortable, unhygienic and there was a limit to the number of layers that could be worn.

To overcome this problem many experiments were carried out using rubber, inflatable tubes, whalebone and cane. One of the earliest inventions was patented by William Thomas and John Marsh in 1849 for a structure composed of India-rubber tubes threaded through hollow lengths of wood to create 'elastic' and 'flexible' hoops.[1] On 23 May 1856 J. Gedge took out a patent for 'crinolines' made of an airtight fabric with 'A small aperture ... for the introduction of the nozzle of a small bellows

for inflating them and a larger aperture for the escape of the air when the wearer wishes to sit down.'[2]

More successful experiments were carried out with steel, such as the design patented by C. Amet in 1856 for 'A crinoline ... made up of a number of covered steel springs ... fastened to strong pieces of tape ... so as to form a "skeleton petticoat".'[3] The use of spring steel made it possible to create a light, pliable, durable and relatively inexpensive crinoline cage. Crinolines, like the one illustrated here, proved effective at distending skirts and released women from the layers of heavy petticoats. Although often ridiculed by the press, they became very popular and were produced in their thousands.

This crinoline cage has the words 'A FAVORITE OF THE EMPRESS' stamped across the waistband. The words probably refer to the Empress Eugénie, wife of Napoleon III, who was fêted for her appearance and fashionable taste in clothes. Such marketing ploys were often used to boost sales and feminize what was essentially a practical garment.

1. Patent no. 12,736, 1849 (British Library)
2. Patent no. 1236, 23 May 1856 (British Library)
3. Patent no. 1729, 22 July 1856 (British Library)

Crinoline cage made of wool and cotton with a spring-steel frame.
British or USA, about 1860
Given by Mrs A. E. Valdez
T.150-1986

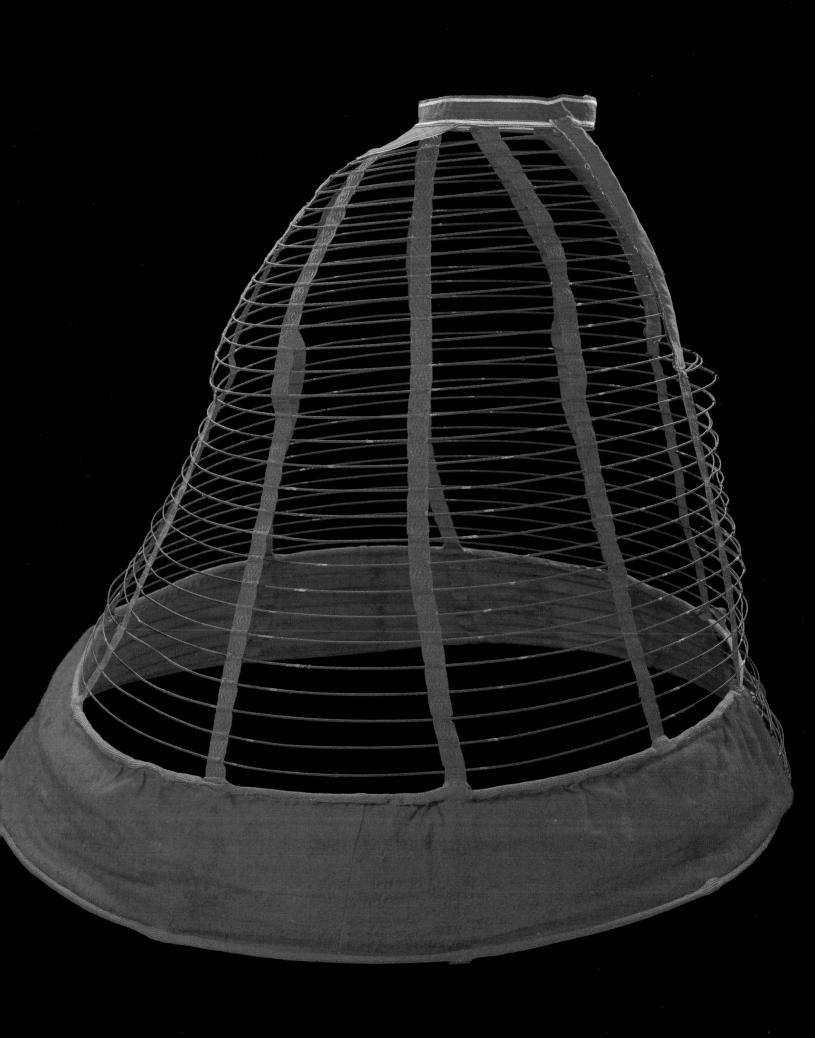

This eye-catching day dress formed part of the trousseau belonging to Miss Janet Gilbert. It is beautifully constructed in the latest style as would befit a young fashionable woman, although its pristine condition suggests that it was never worn. Made of moiré, it has a lustrous rippled sheen accentuated by the rich Prussian blue dye, applied chenille flowers and sparkling metal buttons. Box-pleated trimmings stand out in relief along the bottom edge and seams of the wide pagoda sleeves, emphasizing their width. Had Miss Gilbert worn this dress, white *engageantes* or undersleeves tacked to the armholes would have covered her lower arms and a lace collar might have decorated the neckline.

One of the most striking features of the dress is how the back of the skirt falls in shimmering folds over the dome-shaped petticoat worn underneath. The intense colour and watered pattern of the silk renders any extra trimmings or flounces superfluous. It is composed of ten straight panels of fabric neatly pleated into the waistband to reduce bulk in this area, aided by the pointed bodice which emphasizes the narrow waist. A stiffened skirt lining protects the fabric and gives it more body so that it flows smoothly over the underpinnings without unsightly wrinkles or creases.

Graceful movements and a perfect silhouette were promoted by the introduction of spring-steel hooped petticoats in 1856, often referred to as crinolines. Although frequently ridiculed in the press for their cage-like structure and size, they were also hailed as a blessing. Effective, lightweight, economical and comfortable, they ensured women could wear dresses like this one without having to contend with layers of hot and heavy petticoats. There were drawbacks however, such as danger from fire when the buoyant crinolines passed too close to an open grate and sparks set light to the flammable fabrics. It has been said that the steel framework made it impossible to wrap the victim in a rug to extinguish the flames.

Day dress (bodice and skirt) made of moiré. Bodice trimmed with chenille,
fastened with metal buttons and lined with silk, cotton and whalebone strips.
British, about 1858
Given by Miss Janet Manley
T.90-1964

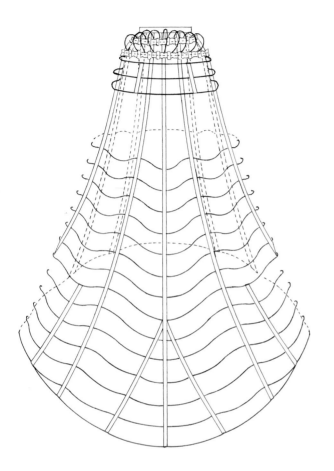
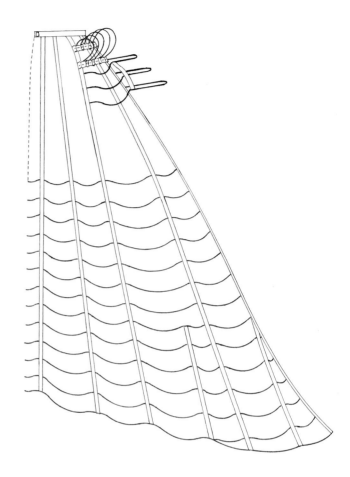

It is not difficult to see why some cage crinolines were known as 'skeleton' petticoats. The undulating bands of spring steel circle the void like a grotesque ribcage. Buoyancy is ensured by the lightness of the steel and the fact that each graduated hoop passes through a stitched opening in the vertical tapes. These tapes are attached to a waistband so that the crinoline sways with the movements of the wearer.

An advertisement in *Illustrated London News* of 1865 extolled the virtues of a similar crinoline:

...so perfect are the wave-like bands that a lady may ascend a steep stair, lean against a table, throw herself into an armchair, pass to her stall at the opera, and occupy a further seat in a carriage, without inconveniencing herself or others, and provoking the rude remarks of observers ... thus modifying, in an important degree, all those peculiarities tending to destroy the modesty of Englishwomen; and lastly, it allows the dress to fall in graceful folds.

Graceful movements were also easier in this style of crinoline as it tended to be smaller than the earlier bell-shaped cages. By 1868 the focus of the skirt had shifted to the back of the body with a distinctive flattening at the front and frequently a slight train at the hemline. To support this silhouette the crinoline diminished in size and, as in this example, sometimes gained a spiral coil of spring steel at the waist to form a bustle.

Cage crinoline made of spring-steel hoops covered in linen.
British, about 1868
Given by Miss C. E. and Miss E. C. Edlmann
T.195-1984

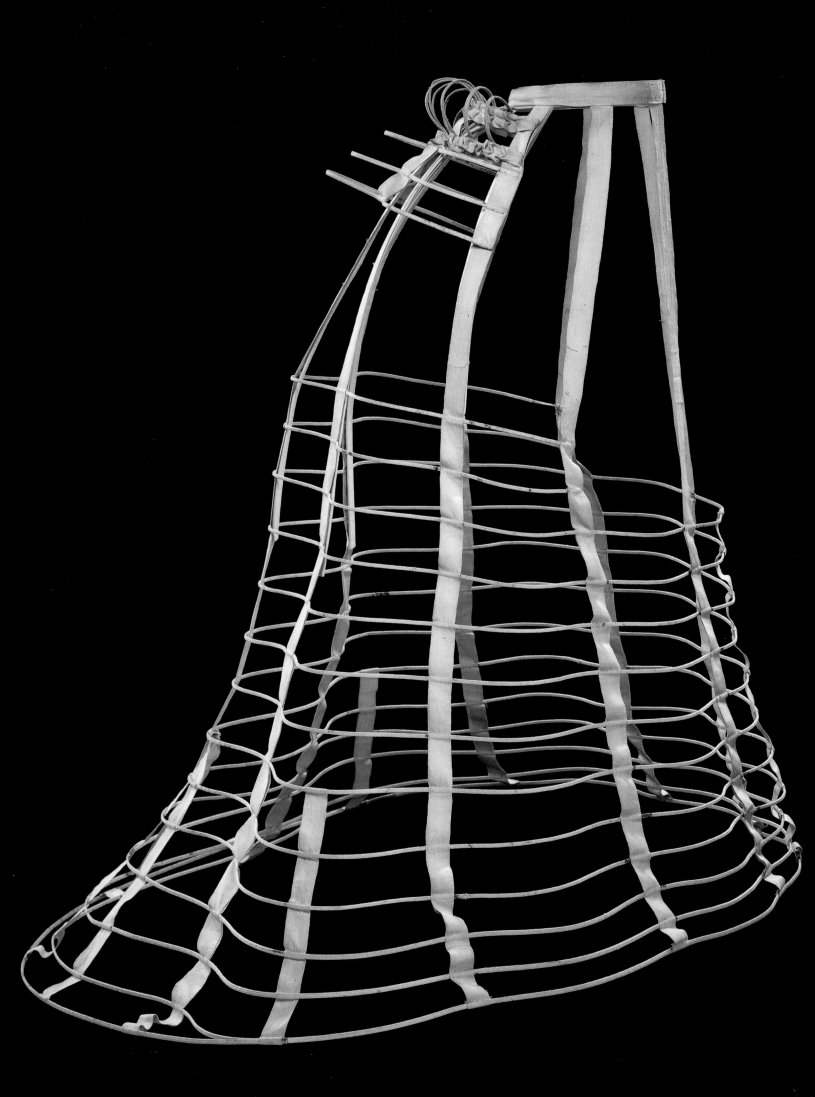

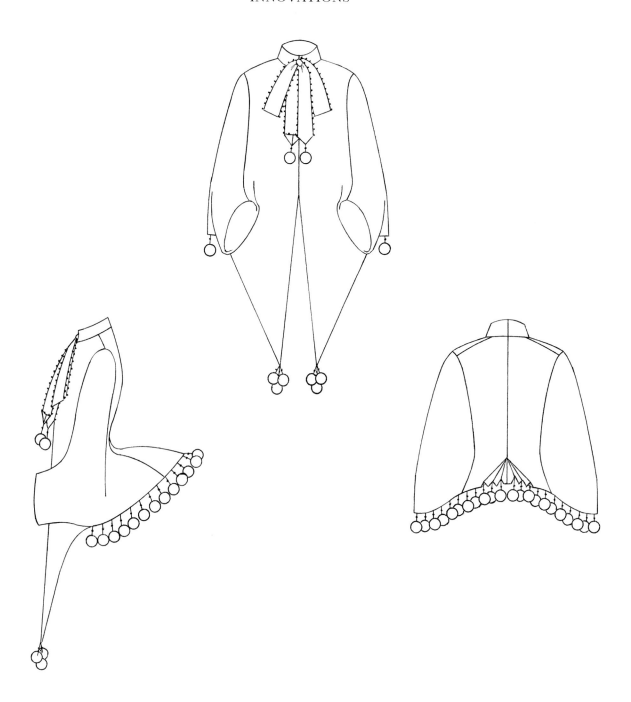

Elegant mantles such as this fanned out over the back of the skirt, displaying the new bustle shape of the mid-1880s to perfection. They were known as dolmans and were characterized by loose, sling-like sleeves cut with the body of the garment so that they resembled half-jacket, half-cape. Dolmans became popular for outdoor wear in the 1870s as their semi-fitted style revealed the shapely contours of the fashionable silhouette. When made of heavier materials such as velvet or fur, they proved ideal for spring and early autumn wear as they were less restricting and cumbersome than a coat. Often worn with a muff, dolmans were also loaded with trimmings, including feathers, ribbons and passementerie.

In this example, padded velvet balls are suspended from knotted silk cords to emphasize the backward projection of the skirt and to trim the ribbon bow fastened at the neck. Crimson balls are also attached to the long tapered ends hanging down the front, which were another typical feature of this style, helping to balance the design.

This dolman was worn by Minnie Fisher, the grandmother of the donor, who was born in 1870 at the Old Rectory, Bathhampton, Bath. Minnie studied at Gloucester School of Art where she won a 'South Kensington prize' for still-life painting. She died in 1963.

Dolman of velvet trimmed with ribbon and lined with crimson silk satin to match the velvet.
British, about 1885
Given by Mrs M. Lawrence
T.299-1983

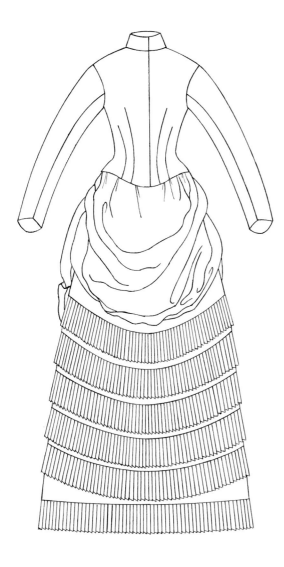

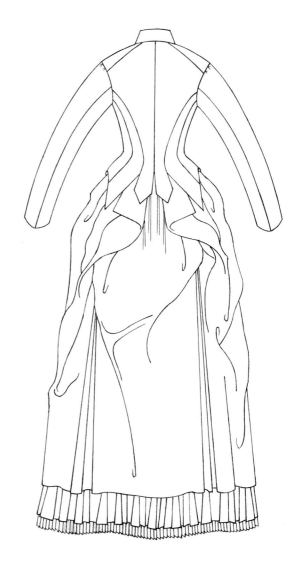

This basqued bodice falls over a perfect cascade of drapery at the back of the skirt to create the fashionable bustled silhouette. The fabric swirls into supple and artistic folds enhanced by the bold design of overlapping circles. Draperies were very popular during the 1880s and included puffed overskirts, swathes of fabric caught up on one side with flowers or ribbon bows, and asymmetrical effects. This made the dresses look complicated, but they were usually composed of separate pieces arranged onto a foundation skirt. This simplified dressmaking and contrasted with previous styles of drapery, which largely depended on skilful cutting and fitting.

The skirt illustrated in this detail is made up of draped and pleated layers of fabric crudely attached to a cotton underskirt, any poor finishing disguised by the trimmings. The back panel is loosely pleated onto the waistband and hangs relatively freely to just above the ruffled hem so that the fabric can be caught with a few stitches to create the drapery. Two long ends cut in the shape of 'burnouse hoods' fan out from the waist to just below the hips, accentuating the backward projection of the skirt.[1] Three seams at the back of the bodice are opened at hip level to form pointed tabs which extend over the bustle.

The concept of the bustle was not new as devices had been used to thrust out the skirt for several hundred years. During the mid-1880s, however, they did reach new and exaggerated proportions, jutting out almost at right angles from the back of the skirt. They came in a huge variety of styles, from crinolettes made of steel half-hoops to down-filled pads and wire mesh structures which folded in on themselves when the wearer sat down. Bustles were often incorporated into the foundation skirt, and in this example four horizontal rows of steel could be inserted into casings stitched onto the lining at the back. When pulled into shape with internal tapes they created the fashionable curved shape.

For more information on this dress see page 148.

1. These appear similar to a description in *Myra's Home Journal of Dress and Fashion*, 1 February 1885: 'small paniers, starting from the point of the corsage, are draped at the back and fall over the pleated skirt in two long ends, like burnouse hoods, tipped with tassels'.

Day dress (bodice and skirt) made of printed cotton stitched onto a cotton foundation skirt.
British, 1885
Given by Miss Agatha Granville
T.7-1926

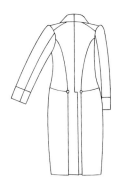

High turn-down collars and broad lapels became fashionable in the early nineteenth century. Cutting them was complicated and tailoring manuals abounded to help pass on this skill. As the author William Power pointed out: 'There is as much art in cutting a collar as in cutting a coat; for if the collar is not properly cut to fit the neck, it easily spoils the fit of the coat over the shoulders, which runs in creases and may roll the lapel and breast from top to bottom.'[1] Several methods were recommended to help avoid these pitfalls. These included stretching and pressing the cloth to prevent a crease under the collar and interlining it with canvas to maintain its form. This example has a square notch and horizontal groove which acts as a decorative device, running parallel with the draw seam on the lapel.[2]

1. William Power, *The Tailor's Scientific Instructor, or Foreman's Unerring Guide in the Art of Cutting* (London, 1845), p.23.

2. This groove resembles a seam but the cloth is not actually cut. Threads are pulled through the cloth to create the channel.

Double-breasted man's tailcoat of superfine partly interlined with felt and fastened with gilt brass buttons.
British, about 1810
Given by F. Gregory
T.355-1903

By the 1850s there were two different types of hunt coat: the dress-hunt coat and the field coat. The field coat tended to be practical and was usually single-breasted and cut in the frock-coat style. Dress coats were double-breasted with short tails instead of skirts. This coat has silk-satin lapel facings and a silk lining throughout, illustrating the finer materials that were used in more formal attire.

Dress coats evolved into a uniform worn exclusively for hunt balls, dinners and club events. Many hunts had membership regulations defining the colour of the coat, collar, revers and buttons. *Baily's Fox-Hunting Directory* of 1897–98, for example, lists the Berkeley Hunt as having a yellow coat, the Dulverton a green plush collar, and the South Union distinctive mauve facings to the evening coat. Dress codes were important, denoting social acceptance into a fashionable hunt as well as individual membership.

For more information on this coat see page 36.

Man's dress coat, made of superfine with gilt brass buttons.
Hampshire Hunt. English, 1860–1900
Given by Harry Helman
T.373-1990

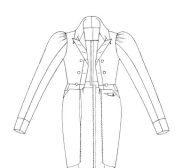

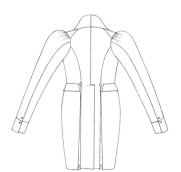

Scarlet became a popular colour for hunting coats in the early nineteenth century. The reasons why red was adopted are uncertain. Some suggest that it commemorated the sport's origins as red was worn by the royal livery for deer-hunting; others that the colour derived from regimental scarlet coats. In all events red was practical as it made the wearer visible to other hunt followers. The colour is often referred to as 'pink' in hunting literature, allegedly after the Mayfair tailor Thomas Pink, who created hunt coats of the finest quality. Not everyone wore red, however. Women generally dressed in dark colours, parsons traditionally wore black, some hunts advocated yellow or green, and a few individuals wore whatever colour they liked.

For more information on this coat see page 156.

Man's field-hunt coat of superfine with gilt brass buttons.
British, 1810–25
Given by Messrs Harrods Ltd
T.772-1913

On this coat a deep notch marks the point where the collar meets the lapel. The unusual cut forms two overlapping points known as a 'thrush's tongue' or 'lark's tongue'. Collar notches were introduced in the early 1800s when high turn-down collars were cut to run into the lapels and many different styles prevailed. The most common design was cut to form the letter 'M', although 'N' and 'V' shapes were also popular. The 'M' cut remained a common device on all coats until about 1855 and on evening dress well into the 1870s.

For more information on this coat see pages 156 and 158.

A man's double-breasted tailcoat of superfine with gilt brass buttons.
British, 1815–20
Given by Lady Osborn
T.118-1953

Double-tongued loops are suspended from this pair of braces. The wearer would pass the bands over his shoulder and attach the leather tabs to four buttons on the front of his trousers. The buckle could be adjusted to vary the height of the loops according to fashion, the size of the individual or taste. The tapered ends with a single buttonhole would be attached behind. This double-tongued design appeared in about 1825 and superseded the earlier style of braces that were fastened with one button on each band, front and back. Throughout the nineteenth century many patents and designs were registered for improvements to the construction of and fastenings for braces, many of which never reached production.

Colourful embroidery became a popular feature on men's braces during the 1840s and 1850s. Small sprays of embroidered red flowers and green and yellow leaves scroll down the bands of this pair. Like many others, they may have been worked by a lady at home as a gift for a lover, friend or relative. Forget-me-knots and roses were popular motifs, although Mr Verdant Green went up to Oxford '... with a pair of braces from Mary, worked with an ecclesiastical pattern of a severe character'.[1]

1. Cuthbert Bede, *The Adventures of Mr Verdant Green, an Oxford Freshman* (London,1853), p.15.

Man's braces of canvas and leather, embroidered with wool and lined with silk.
British, 1840s–50s
Given by Mr A. H. Prior
T.91-1971

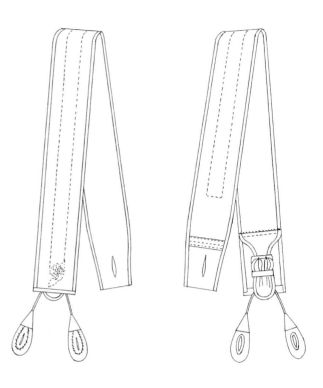

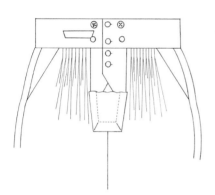

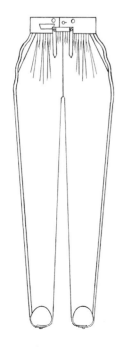

Buttoned tabs, known as 'trowser straps' or 'anchor straps', protrude from the bottom edge of this pair of trousers. They were introduced in about 1820 and, when fastened, anchored the trouser legs under the boot or shoe, keeping them taut. To enhance the effect, an arch is cut into the fabric over the instep through which the foot could project without causing unsightly creases in the silk. The trouser bottoms, like the straps, are lined with linen for extra reinforcement, as this part of the garment would take a lot of strain.

One of the problems with this style of 'trowser strap' was the rigidity of the materials, which did not allow for much movement of the foot. The strap also passed under the sole of the boot or shoe, greatly exposing it to wear and dirt. Early patent records are full of designs to try and remedy these evils, such as hooking straps onto metal studs fixed to the edges of the sole, fitting spring mechanisms, and using elastic webbing to provide more flexibility.

This style of trousers was known as 'Cossacks'. They became popular around 1814 and were inspired by the trousers worn by Cossack cavalry regiments during the Napoleonic wars.[1] Fashionable Cossack trousers were generously cut and the excess fabric at the top was pleated into the waistband and front falls. By the date of this pair they tended to taper towards the ankles, which required skilful positioning of striped or patterned fabric along the side-seams.

1. The Russian cavalry included the famous Cossacks who wore both their traditional dress as well as a full dress uniform

Man's 'Cossack' trousers of silk lined with linen.
British, 1820s
Given by Mr Frederick Gill
T.197-1914

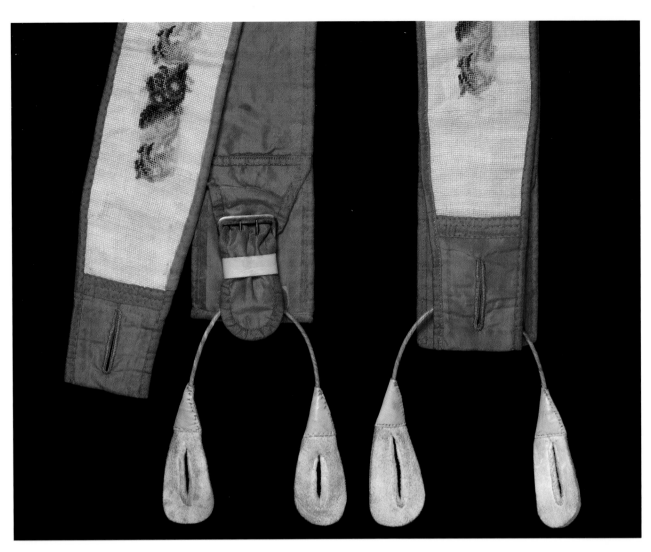

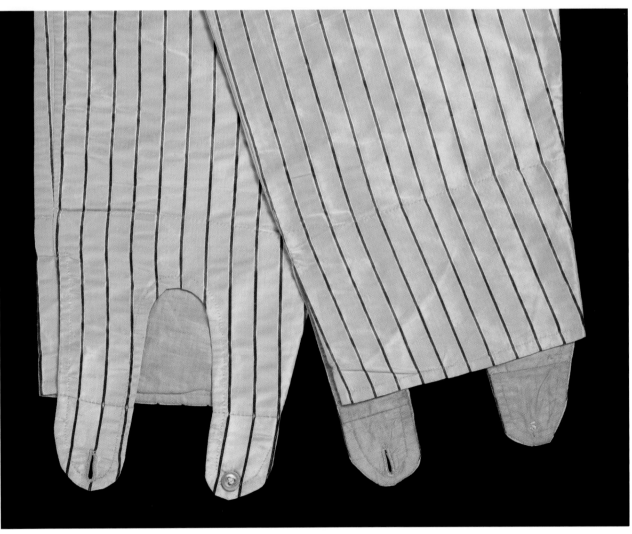

A metal buckle passes through a strap on the back of this waist-coat. The waistcoat can therefore be adjusted to suit the size of the wearer and create the fashionable 'nipped in' look at the waist. Many manufacturers and individuals devised improved waistcoat fastenings during the 1830s and 1840s, some made of metal, others incorporating elastic. There was much competition, and innovators sought to safeguard their designs through a registration process. In 1839 the Design Copyright Act was passed in which a sample, model or illustration was deposited with the registrar of the Board of Trade. The name and address of the owner was recorded and the design was allocated a registration number which protected it for a set period.

The words 'IMPROVED BUCKLE FOR VESTS, WELCH, MARGETSON & CO. LONDON' are printed onto the back of this waistcoat. This indicates that the buckle was a registered design. Welch, Margetson & Co. was a London clothing firm specializing in men's wear, including shirts, collars, handkerchiefs, waistcoats, neckcloths and braces. It would clearly have an interest in protecting its designs from competitors as well as marketing its products as superior and innovative. In 1841 and 1848 the founders of the firm, Joseph James Welch and John Stewart Margetson, took out two registered designs for buckles.[1] It is likely that one of these is the design for this waistcoat fastening.

1. Registered design no. 671, 19 April 1841. Registered design no. 53776, 7 August 1848 (The National Archives, London).

Man's waistcoat of jacquard-woven silk with a cotton back. The base of the foreparts are lined with leather.
Welch, Margetson & Co. Cheapside, London, 1848–50
Given by the Misses Spiers
T.3-1917

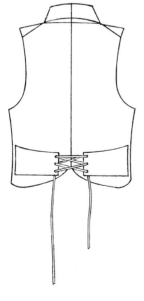

The words 'METALLIC OILET HOLES, WELCH & MARGETSON, Patentees' are emblazoned on the back of this waistcoat. 'Oilet' refers to the six metal reinforced holes threaded with cotton tape, rather like the lacing on a corset. This type of waistcoat fastening was a popular alternative to the strap and buckle design (see above). They were also known as eyelets, and oilets is the earlier term, derived from the French *oeillet*.

An interesting marketing ploy is revealed by the reference to 'Patentees'. This suggests that the clothing firm Welch & Margetson had invented these eyelets and taken out a patent, which gave it the right to manufacture them without competition. There is, however, no record in any of the British or French specifications of any patent being issued to either Joseph James Welch or John Stewart Margetson for this product. The earliest patent they received was for the manufacture of 'travelling cases' and 'wrappers' in 1853.[1] It is therefore likely that the firm was using its status as a patent holder to market other goods such as back fastenings for waistcoats.

Metal eyelets were first invented by Thomas Rogers in March 1823[2] and were inserted into stays and boots to reinforce the fabric and assist with lacing by having a smooth inner surface. They proved much stronger than the ordinary sewn eyelets and were soon used on a wide range of garments, including waistcoats.

1. Patent no. 17 (British Library).
2. Patent no. 4766 (British Library).

Man's waistcoat of jacquard-woven silk with a cotton back. The base of the foreparts are lined with leather.
Welch & Margetson. Cheapside, London, about 1853
Given by Mrs Tilly
T.293-1973

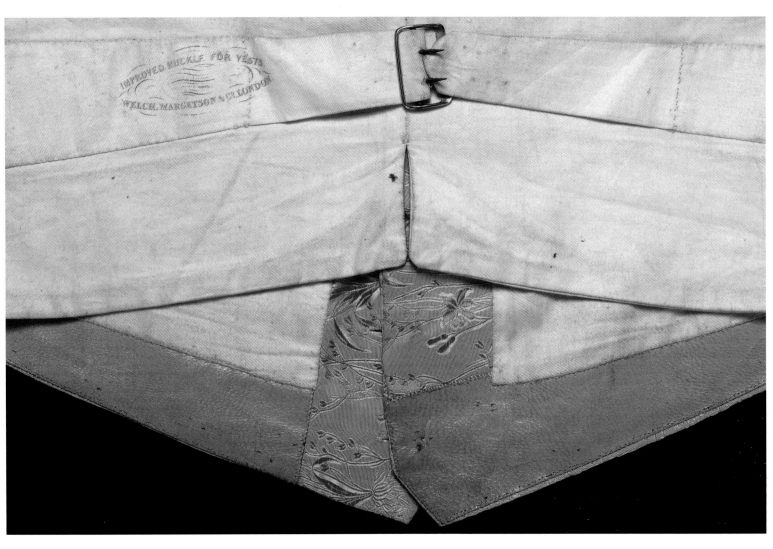

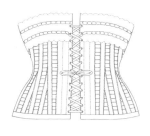

An elegant steel busk accentuates the curves of this corset. Narrow at the top, dipping in at the waist and widening out over the abdomen, the style was introduced in about 1873. Its distinctive shape was heralded as an important innovation, increasing comfort, preserving health, reducing unsightly bulges and enhancing the figure. It appeared on fashionable models until the 1890s and was known by imaginative names such as the 'spoon', 'pear', 'envelope' and 'patent taper' busk.

'Brown's Patent Dermathistic No. 2076 R/D. 1883' is stamped in purple on the lining of the busk. Dermathistic corsets had bones, busks and steels protected by leather and were promoted as elegant, durable, scientifically constructed and comfortable. An advertisement in *The Young Ladies' Journal* of 1894 announced: 'Experienced dressmakers find they can easily fit bodices to perfection over these corsets. Try them and you will never wear any other kind.'

For more information on this corset see page 170.

Corset of red sateen with bone channels, busk and centre back steels covered in leather. Machine-sewn.
British, 1883–95
T.84-1980

A double layer of vertical tapes has been skilfully stitched onto a foundation of horizontal cotton bands to create this elegant corset. The vertical tapes form channels for the whalebone strips, which were then secured into place with bound edges. The whalebone insertions fan out over the bust and hips, helping to create the fashionable curvaceous silhouette. This type of design was known as a 'ventilated' corset and was suitable for sports and summer wear. The spaces in between the whalebone and cotton tapes were intended to allow air to circulate, enabling the skin to 'exhale' and perspiration to evaporate. This was one of the many 'health' innovations endorsed by manufacturers of late nineteenth-century underwear.

As awareness increased of the damage caused by wearing corsets, many attempts were made to modify construction and spurious claims were frequently advertized to boost sales.

Corset made of whalebone and cotton trimmed with broderie anglaise and silk ribbon. Front-fastening busk, slot-and-stud fastening and centre back supports made of steel.
British, 1890–1900
Given by Miss S. P. Emery
T.184-1962

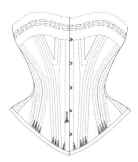
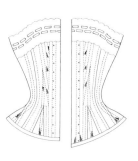

Fashion and technological innovation changed the shape of late nineteenth-century corsets. As the bustle replaced the crinoline and bodices contoured the figure, corsets became longer to achieve the desired hourglass silhouette. They encased the abdomen and enveloped the hips, and the amount of whalebone also increased to give a smoother outline and help prevent wrinkling of the fabric. This corset from the 1880s is composed of twelve separate shaped pieces and forty whalebone strips.

To improve shape, performance and comfort, manufacturers claimed numerous inventions. One of the most successful was the steam-moulding process developed by Edwin Izod in 1868, and still used in the 1880s to create elegant corsets such as this one. The procedure involved placing a corset, wet with starch, on a steam-heated copper torso form until it dried into shape. The result was a beautifully formed corset, whereby 'the fabric and bones are adapted with marvellous accuracy to every curve and undulation of the finest type of figure'.[1]

1. *The Ladies' Gazette of Fashion* advertisement (London, July 1879).

'Izod's Patent Moulded Sewn Corset' of satin with metal slot-and-stud fastening, hand-flossing and a woven silk braid trimming. Lined with coutil.
Edwin Izod. English, 1887
Given by Miss Benjamin and worn at her wedding in 1887
T.265-1960

Improvements in design, equipment and materials meant that corsets could mould the figure to suit the latest fashions. The straight busk on this corset creates a vertical line from bust to abdomen which complemented the less rounded, more angular silhouette of the 1890s. It was also supposed to relieve pressure on the internal organs while supporting the stomach. Shaped pieces (five on each side) have been seamed together and bust and hip gussets inserted to give the corset its distinctive shape. Strips of whalebone follow the contours of the hourglass silhouette, creating a rigid structure to emphasize the smallness of the waist. Each strip is enclosed in a bone channel formed by neat rows of machine-stitching. The decorative embroidery stitches (flossing) visible towards the bottom and back of the corset prevent the whalebone from forcing its way out of these channels. A hook is attached at the centre front to prevent the petticoat from riding up and causing extra bulk at the waist.

For more information on this corset see page 118.

Corset of pink satin trimmed with hand-made bobbin lace. Machine-sewn with hand-flossing and metal slot-and-stud fastening.
British, early 1890s
T.738-1974

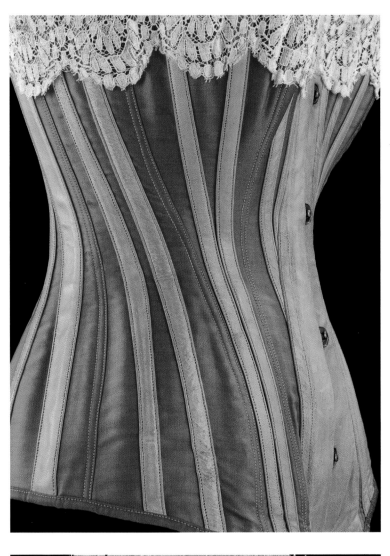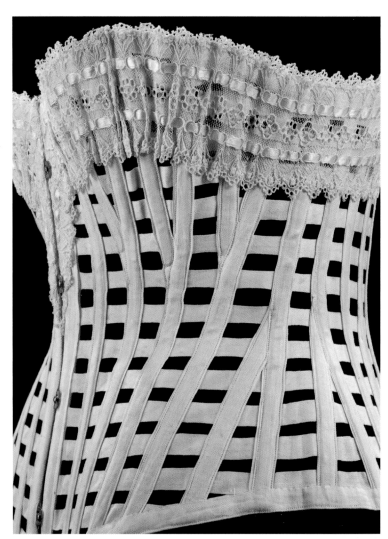
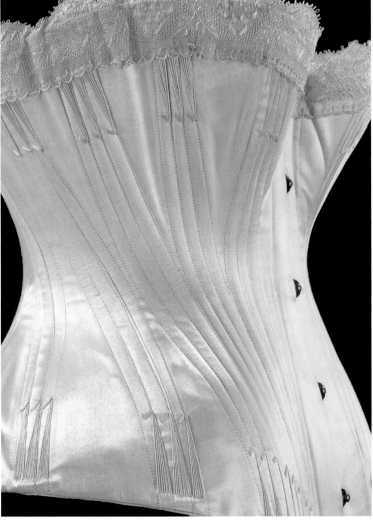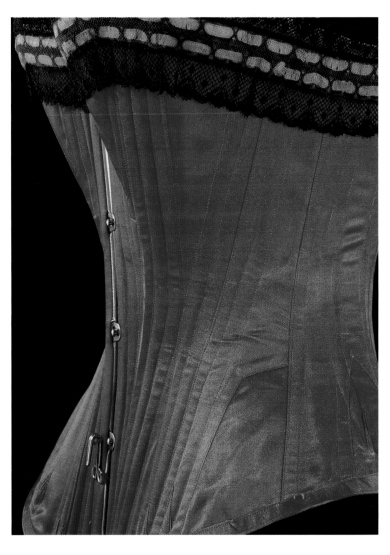

Machine-net dresses provided an ideal ground for richly textured embroidery. In this example, pink chenille rosebuds and linked leaves stand out in relief against the red net, blooming into full-blown roses on the sleeves and around the hem. The simple construction of the dress and self-bound seams ensure that nothing detracts from these harmonious effects.

Chenille floral motifs were not in themselves new as they had appeared on eighteenth-century embroidered and woven garments for men and women. They became a particularly fashionable feature of women's gowns, aprons, scarves and hats in about 1807. Roses were popular, but other flowers such as lilies and nasturtiums also emerged, their colours usually complementing that of the net or underdress. When combined with delicate gold jewellery, satin shoes and hair dressed in ringlets, the overall impression must have been enchanting.

Evening dress made of machine-made silk bobbin net, hand-embroidered with chenille thread in a variety of straight stitches. Fastened with silk satin ribbon (the silk underdress is a replica).
British, 1807–11
Given by Mrs George Atkinson
T.194-1958

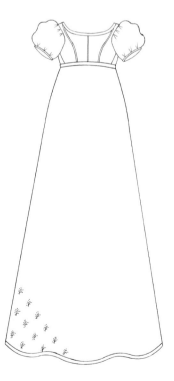

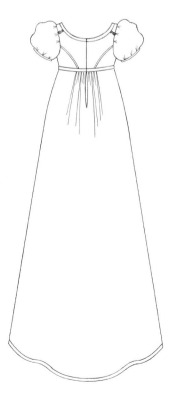

Sprigs embroidered with spangles and silver-gilt braid adorn this delicate evening dress. It is made of machine-made bobbin net which would have glided over the silk satin underdress worn beneath. Elaborate gowns like this one were saved for special occasions such as dances and balls. The thin, gauzy materials created a dreamy look, and gold thread or sparkling beads and spangles glittered in the artificial light of the dancing room. These light materials also prevented the wearer from getting too hot in stuffy, overcrowded spaces.

Net dresses were very fashionable and their popularity was spurred by new inventions. The development of machine-made net in the late eighteenth and early nineteenth centuries meant that gauzy lace effects were increasingly affordable either as trimmings or entire coverings. The bobbin-net machine was patented by the Englishman John Heathcoat in 1808 and produced a superior net identical to the twist-net grounds of hand-made bobbin lace. It was so successful that women in the highest ranks of society, including Napoleon's first wife, the Empress Josephine, wore machine-net dresses. Initially, however, all machine nets were plain and had to be embroidered by hand.

Evening dress made of machine-made silk bobbin net, hand-embroidered with silver-gilt braid and spangles. Seams bound with silk satin (the silk underdress is a replica).
British, about 1810
Given by Messrs Harrods Ltd
T.795-1913

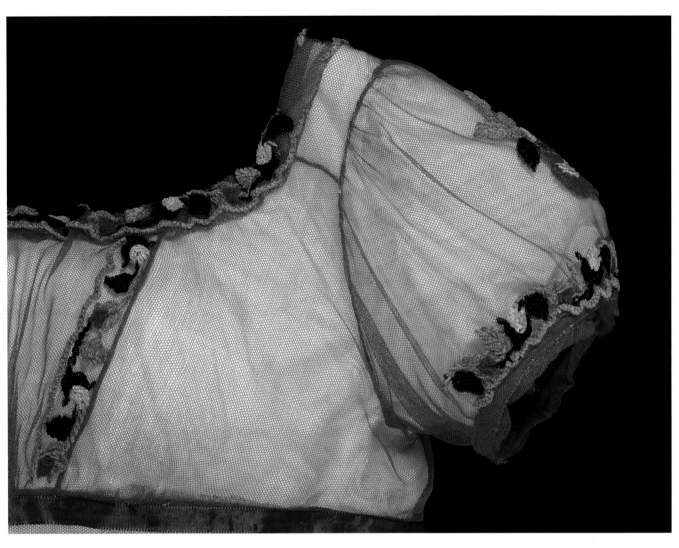

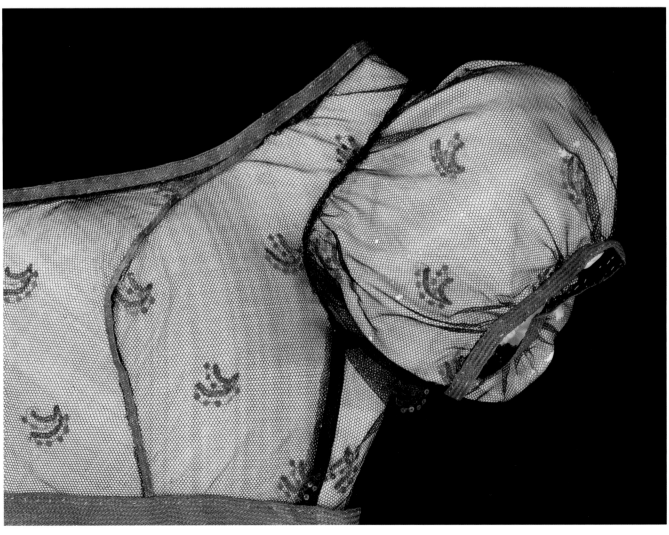

A short puffed overskirt creates elaborate draped effects on this fashionable walking costume. The fabric is gathered into pre-arranged folds to resemble eighteenth-century polonaise gowns and 1860s dresses, which were looped up by a variety of devices, including silk cords and concealed drawstrings. Draperies were very popular during the 1880s, and pleats, poufs, gathers, panniers, swags and asymmetrical effects produced a great fullness around the hips, making the waist appear very slender.

Such imaginative trimmings show how one of the major innovations in nineteenth-century dressmaking, the sewing machine, encouraged the use of complex decoration. Although it could stitch much faster than a hand-sewer and was generally employed in running up long seams, some of the time saved seemed to go into lavish arrangements of folds and pleats. In this example, the seams and gathering at the back of the skirt are machine-stitched, whereas the drapery effects and finishing are carried out by hand.

Its development was the result of several inventions, culminating in Elias J. Howe's (1819–67) patent of 1846 for a lock-stitch machine. This is seen as a milestone in the development of the sewing machine industry as it used a curved, grooved needle with an eye as well as two threads, thereby creating a much stronger stitch. Successive improvements by a pool of patent holders led to the introduction of machined clothing production during the 1850s.

Walking dress (bodice, skirt and overskirt) of printed cotton.
British, about 1883
Given by Mrs Gibbs
T.254-1928

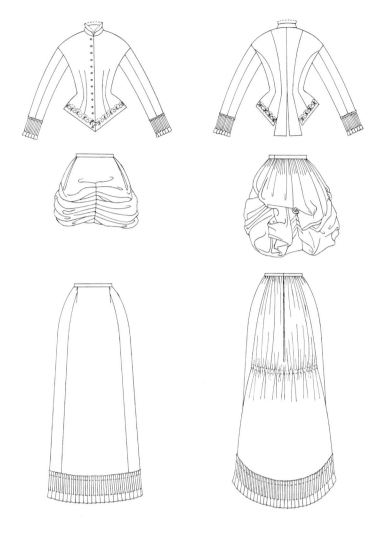

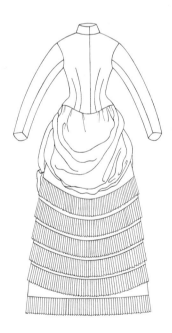
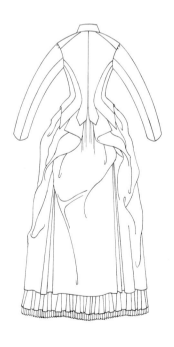

Pleated ruffles are machine-sewn onto the front panel of this skirt to give the impression of a multi-layered garment. The pleats are so regular and the fabric so striking that from a distance the trimmings and skirt fabric blend into each other and the joins are barely visible. They illustrate how in some respects the sewing machine saved time and labour, as such decoration could be applied much quicker than if stitched by hand. Many of the more complicated arrangements of material were still carried out by hand, and sewers also tended to hand-finish fashionable garments.

The swathe of fabric at the top of this skirt was known as scarf drapery and it created a simulated overskirt when pulled up and pleated into the side seams. This has been arranged onto a cotton foundation skirt by hand, as has the bustled drapery at the back of the garment.

For more information on this dress see page 136.

Day dress (bodice and skirt) made of printed cotton stitched onto a cotton foundation skirt.
British, 1885
Given by Miss Agatha Granville
T.7-1926

This machine-knitted woman's vest was displayed at the Great Exhibition of 1851, held in the specially constructed 'Crystal Palace' in Hyde Park, London. This was the first 'world fair' and its aim was to celebrate excellence in trade, industry, education and design. Both machine- and hand-made objects were displayed and the 'Juries' reporting on the exhibits considered machine-knitting particularly significant. Knitwear was an important British industry, but methods of production were often antiquated. By the early 1850s, however, enterprizing manufacturers were beginning to revolutionize the trade by using steam-powered machinery.

Much of the knitwear exhibited showed advances in design and improvements in manufacturing techniques. This fully-fashioned vest was cleverly shaped to accommodate the female figure so that it did not bunch up under the arms or at the waist in an uncomfortable manner. It was possibly made by John Lart and Son from Nottingham, who were given 'Honourable Mention' by the Juries for 'clothing fashioned to fit the bust and waist of the wearer'.[1]

1. *The Exhibition Jury reports*, Vol. III, p.1052.

Woman's machine-knitted vest made of wool with cotton placket and mother-of-pearl buttons.
British, 1851
T.55-1959

Dr Gustav Jaeger's doctrines on sanitary clothing[1] are epitomized in this woollen corset. He believed that the wearing of linen, cotton and silk was injurious to health as they chilled the skin, quickly became saturated with perspiration and absorbed noxious vapours from the body. Wool, on the other hand, was porous, allowing perspiration to pass freely away, leaving the skin dry and warm. For these reasons he advocated that all garments, even shoes, should be made of untreated, undyed wool.

Dr Jaeger promoted a range of clothing, including the 'Sanitary Woollen Corset' which was supposedly healthier and more comfortable than many fashionable models. He did not oppose the wearing of corsets but criticized tight lacing and the materials used to construct them. This example is made from undyed wool and is reinforced with vertical rows of string cording, making it less restrictive than a fully boned corset. Pleated insertions gently define the bust and adjustable shoulder straps reduce pressure on the waist.

1. Gustav Jaeger, *Dr Jaeger's essays on Health-Culture* (London, 1887).

'Sanitary Woollen Corset' made of undyed wool with steel busk, whalebone and mother-of-pearl buttons.
The Jaeger Co. Ltd. London, 1890–1900
Bequeathed and worn by Miss E. J. Bowden (1881–1968)
T.229-1968

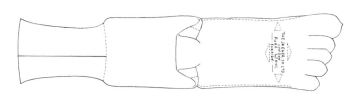

Five-toed socks were especially recommended for those with perspiring feet. Dr Jaeger claimed that 'The interposition ... of a layer of woollen material between each toe absorbs the perspiration and rapidly effects a remarkable-change. The skin between the toes becomes dry and wholesome, soft corns disappear, and the squeezed, crippled appearance of the toes greatly alters for the better.'[1] He also argued that they enhanced circulation of the blood 'over the whole body' by keeping the extremities warm.

This sock is knitted like the fingers of a glove, with a separate 'receptacle' for each toe. To reduce bulk the socks were made of a thinner yarn than was conventional and the big toe was larger than the other digits. As a concession to fashionable dress, the

areas of the foot and heel flap, which would have been visible when wearing shoes, are black. Jaeger believed that dark colours were less healthy than light as they absorbed more heat, leading to increased perspiration and discomfort. But as men's suits tended to be dark, particularly for winter wear, white socks would not have been acceptable.

1. Gustav Jaeger, *Dr Jaeger's essays on Health-Culture* (London, 1887), p.123.

Man's 'Sanitary Woollen Sock' made of machine-knitted wool.
The Jaeger Co. Ltd. London, 1890–1910
Given by Jane Waller
T.395-2001

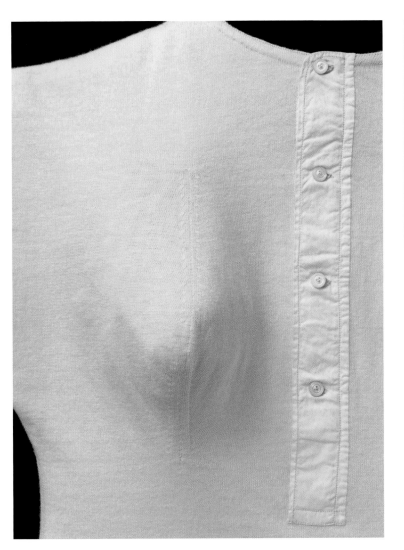

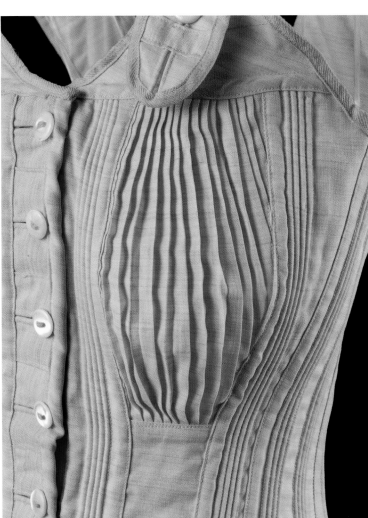

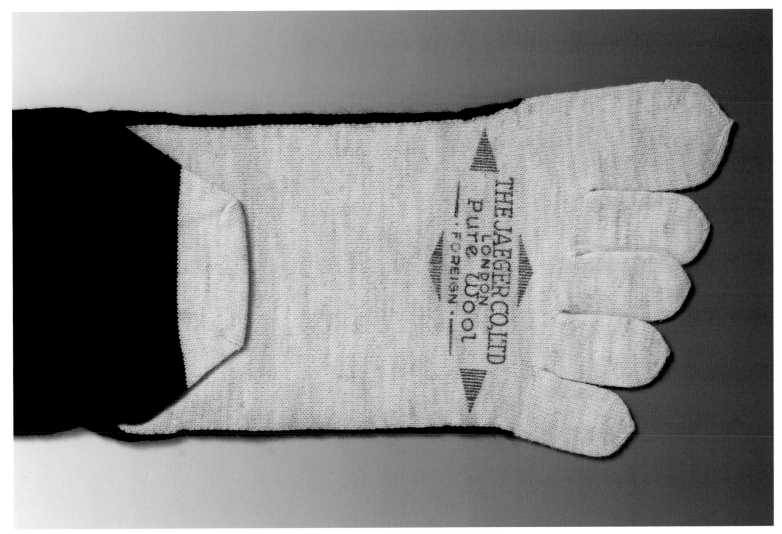

Construction
Details

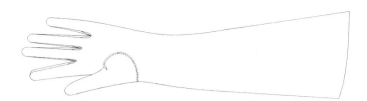

In the early nineteenth century a lady's toilette was not complete without gloves, and she was regarded as improperly dressed if she left the house ungloved. For both sexes gloves were available in a wide range of colours, and the illustration gives us a glimpse of the vibrancy of those colours. An indispensable accessory for day and evening wear, ladies would have many pairs of gloves suited to different occasions and chosen to match particular outfits. However, a strict etiquette applied to the wearing of gloves, and if a lady was in mourning she was limited to the choice of black only, or to white for the second period of mourning. It was also considered extremely bad form to wear discoloured, grubby or worn gloves, and some of the paler coloured fine leather or suede gloves might only have been worn once.

The image shows a detail of an elegant elbow-length evening glove of bright yellow kid, a highly fashionable colour in the early

nineteenth century. The pattern is cut with a 'Bolton thumb' and with quirks and fourchettes to the fingers. Each glove has 'pique' or 'lapseams' and is hand-sewn with minute stitches using a white silk thread. The same thread is used for a double line of decorative stitching around the base of the thumb and to work the double lines of stitching for the long 'points' on the back of the glove. The glove does not have a wrist opening, but the exquisitely fine, soft leather would easily have stretched to allow for the glove to be put on and carefully eased onto the fingers and up the arm. M. K.

One of a pair of elbow-length evening gloves of bright yellow ultra fine kid leather.
Probably French, 1820s–30s
Circ.175-1917

A gentleman was also expected to be gloved, and the cut and style of the blue glove is typical of the period 1860–80. It is made of calf leather and cut with a 'Bolton thumb', quirks and fourchettes. The glove is hand-sewn with seams finely oversewn using a contrasting white silk thread. Simple and elegant detailing is given by the double row of white tambour stitching to the points and the narrow white leather edge-binding to finish the cuff. The glove is wrist length and without a fastening which was the fashion at the time. The long lines of pointing on the backs which extend almost to the finger stitching are also typical of the

period. Gloves of this date were designed to be close fitting, and the knuckle marks and bulges caused by the finger ends show that this glove has been worn and used prior to its acquisition as a museum object.
M. K.

Man's glove of blue calf leather.
British, 1860s–80s
Gift of Mrs Edith Renouf
T.32-1922

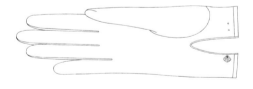

The elegant and high-quality lady's green kid leather dress glove dating from 1860–80 is very similar in style to the blue calf leather gentleman's glove also illustrated. The glove is cut with a 'French thumb', which includes a thumb quirk and fourchettes to the fingers but no finger quirks. The glove is machine-sewn in green silk with overseams. The dainty and elegant long points are also machine-sewn in green silk. The glove is finished with a narrow band of contrasting white kid applied to the wrist edge as a binding. There is a small gilt metal shell-shaped fastening on the inside of the wrist with two fixings for this fastening to

hook onto. Ladies' gloves of the late nineteenth century were very close fitting and the use of this fastening served to pull the glove tightly into the wrist, giving a smooth line.
M. K.

Woman's glove of green kid leather with small gilt metal shell-shaped fastening. An oval label inside the glove is stamped with 'Gartier'.
French or British, 1860–80
T.101-1935

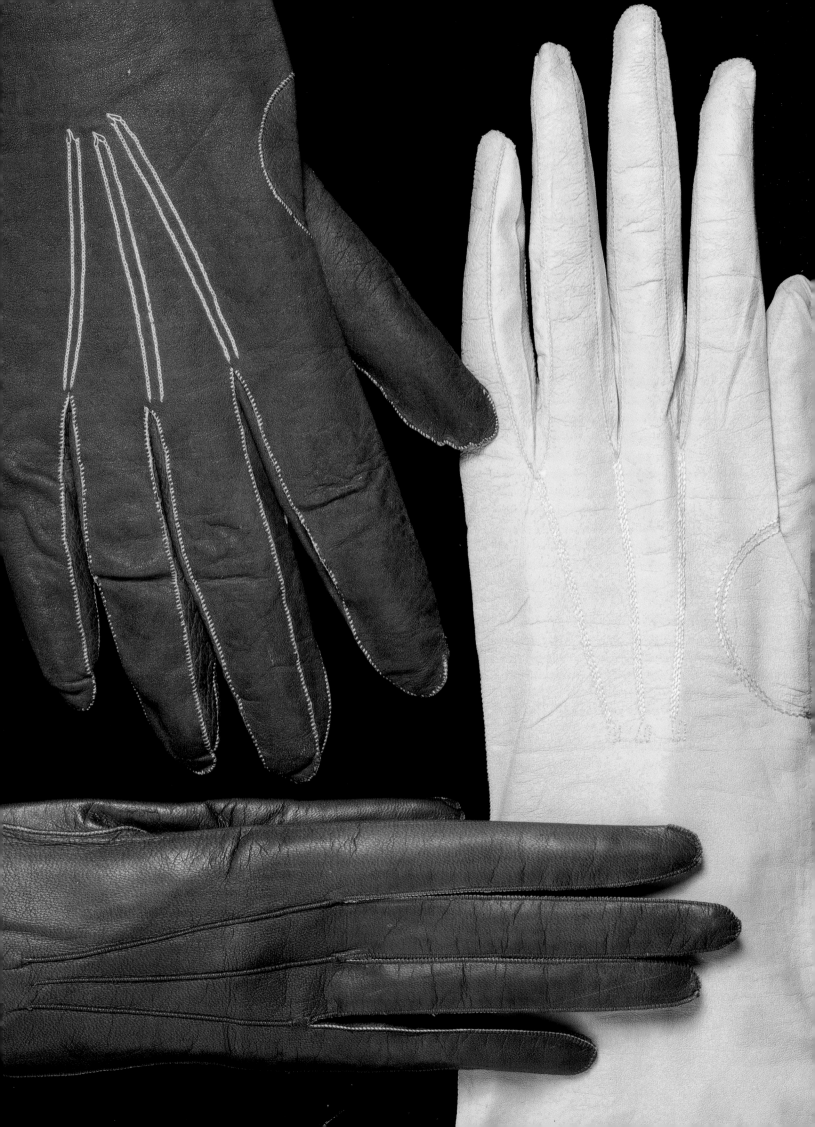

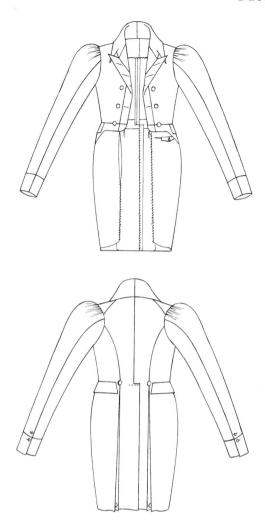

The back of this tail coat reveals a range of pockets, some purely decorative, others hidden. Two rectangular flaps flank the centre back vent as was fashionable during this period, but the pockets are 'blind', probably to discourage pickpockets. The real pocket is concealed in the skirt lining. There are two further pockets inside the back pleats, a feature that started to appear on men's coats at the beginning of the century. It is likely that they would have held something slim such as gloves or a handkerchief, so as not to disturb the line of the cloth.

Although fashion dictated certain styles, finer details such as the number and design of pockets could be varied according to the whim of the tailor or the customer's wishes. There was also less focus on the appearance of the lining, and tailors often patched these together using scraps of cloth left over from cutting.

For more information on this coat see pages 138 and 158.

Man's double-breasted tail coat of superfine with gilt brass buttons.
British, 1815–20
Given by Lady Osborn
T.118-1953

Fox-hunting involves galloping across open country, jumping fences and hedges, often in bad weather. The tails of cutaway coats would inevitably rise behind the rider, as befell the Surtees' character Mr Jorrocks: 'Down Windy-lane … we distinctly recognize the worthy master of the pack, followed by Jorrocks, with his long coat-laps floating in the breeze.'[1] This detail shows a back pocket which is carefully constructed so that nothing would fall out. It is very deep, concealed under the flap of the coat and fastened with a tab and button for extra security. In combining practicality with elegance the tailor has demonstrated his skills.

The cut of the coat was also important to ensure a neat, close-fitting line. The sporting writer Nimrod tended to take smartness a little too literally, but his comments on a follower of the Quorn hunt indicate the importance of correct dress: 'When turned out at the hands of his valet, he presents the *beau idéal* of his *caste*. The exact Stultz-like fit of his coat, his superlatively well-cleaned leather breeches and boots cannot be matched elsewhere.'[2]

For more information on this coat see page 138.

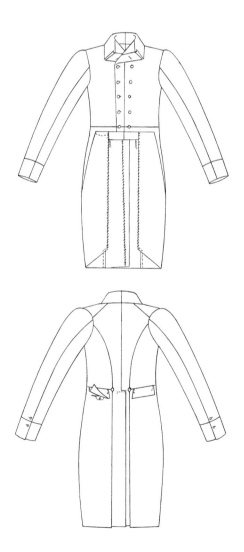

1. R.S. Surtees, *Jorrocks' Jaunts and Jollities* (First published 1838; this edition London, 1949), p.17.
2. Charles James Apperley (Nimrod) cited in Raymond Carr, *English Fox-Hunting – A History* (London, 1986), p.136.

Man's field-hunt coat of superfine with gilt brass buttons and cotton pocket linings.
British, 1810–25
Given by Messrs Harrods Ltd
T.772-1913

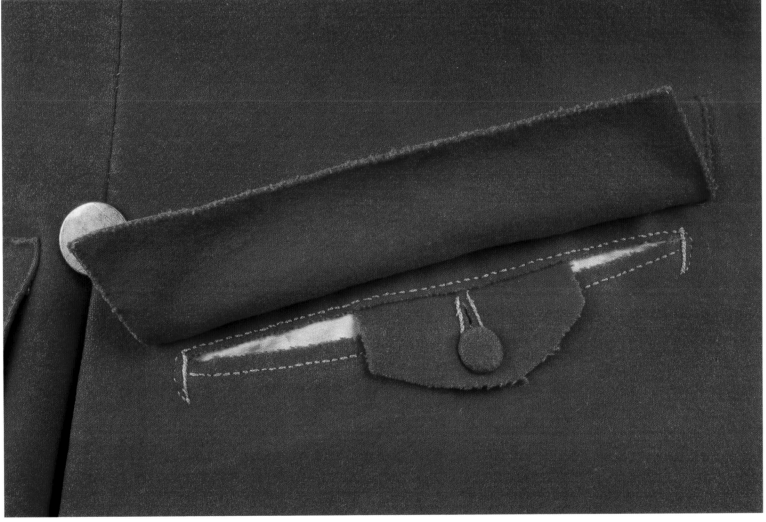

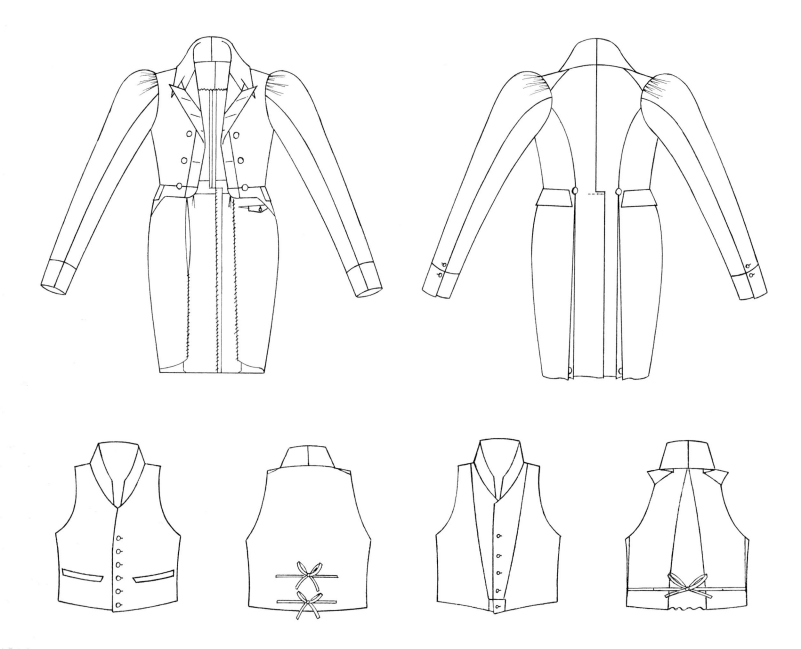

British tailors were renowned for their skill in manipulating woollen cloth. During the early nineteenth century, scores of tailors, cutters and draughtsmen promoted a variety of methods and measuring systems to improve coat-cutting. One of the most significant developments was the invention of the tape measure, which was in general use by 1818. Although several tailors claimed credit for its introduction, it may have been inspired by the inch measurements taken by shoemakers. The tape measure revolutionized tailoring as it meant that tailors could take swift and accurate dimensions of a customer. Previously they had had to rely on unwieldy slips of parchment paper which were held up to the body and snipped to designate the various lengths and widths.

With the correct measurements a tailor could set about chalking, marking and cutting the cloth. Once this was done the coat could be made up then pressed and stretched into shape with a variety of irons and a damp cloth. The coat shown here demonstrates the tailor's skill as it shows off the figure to its full advantage. He could cut the coat to conceal human imperfections, focusing the eye instead on symmetry and proportion. The high turn-down collar, narrow shoulders, close-fitting sleeves, broad lapels and nipped-in waist emphasize the grace and elegance of the human form. The foreparts sit close to the body but without undue tightness, revealing a brightly coloured waistcoat, under-waistcoat, frilled shirt and cravat.

For more information on this coat see pages 138 and 156.

Man's tailcoat of superfine with gilt brass buttons, worn over a yellow poplin
waistcoat and pink silk and cotton under-waistcoat (the cravat is a replica).
British, 1815–20
Given by Lady Osborn (coat), G. J. Lamb (waistcoat), Miss E. M. Coulson (under-waistcoat)
T.118-1953, T.51-1958, T.153-1931

Circular pads shape the bust of this bodice lining. They were formed by placing a round piece of wadding over the canvas interlining, which was often constructed with darts to fit the form of the breasts. Careful manipulation of the canvas by stretching and shrinking the cloth with an iron also helped mould it to the figure. To give further structure to the riding habit, whalebone supports were usually inserted along the vertical seams of the bodice. Once this was done the tailor neatly covered the interlining, seams, boning and wadding with a silk lining and quilted the padding in concentric circles.

This lining shows how the construction of tailored bodices differed from those of the dressmaker. The latter usually fitted the lining first and then covered it with the outer material of the garment. The tailor followed the reverse method, fitting the outside first and then inserting the lining to create a neater finish. Tailoring techniques were well suited to the production of woollen garments such as riding outfits, jackets, coats and cycling costumes.

The internal construction of a woman's tailored riding bodice (forepart with buttons also visible) made of superfine lined with silk twill, canvas and whalebone strips.
British, about 1900
Given by Mrs Morison
T.158-1962

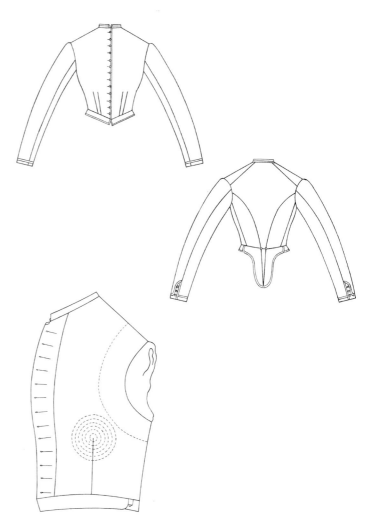

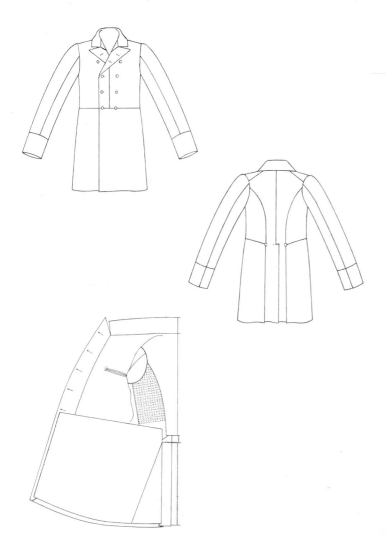

The structure of a coat could enhance a figure or highlight its defects. Sartorial elegance depended on precise measuring, accurate cutting and careful construction to conceal defects such as sloping shoulders, while highlighting positive attributes. This was particularly true of the frock coat, which was considered 'the garment above all others that displays the tailor's skill, and pays for the high class workmanship bestowed in its production'.[1]

During the second half of the nineteenth century, improved construction techniques helped shape the perfect coat to suit the individual as well as his fashionable or personal tastes. Great attention was paid to building up or toning down the figure at key points such as the chest, shoulders and back. In this example, wadding graded to shape has been placed around the scye (armhole) and down the sides. The silk that covers it was creased into squares with an iron and caught at the corners with prick stitches. This helped to create a smooth line at the back of the coat round the shoulder blades, and a neat lining to cover up technical imperfections.

1. W.D.F. Vincent, *The Cutter's Practical Guide to Cutting Part II* (London, c.1895), p.29.

The internal construction of a man's frock coat. Superfine lined with silk satin with striped silk and cotton sleeve linings and a canvas interlining.
Irish, 1890–99
Given by A. W. Furlong
T.47-1947

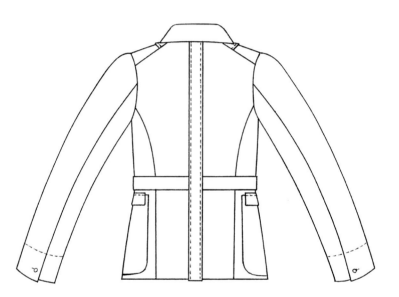

The Norfolk jacket was a versatile garment worn for a range of leisure pursuits. It was a modified version of the 'Norfolk' shirt, a comfortable box-pleated jacket popular for shooting in the 1860s. The style was allegedly designed in the mid-nineteenth century for the Duke of Norfolk, to be worn on his estate. During the 1880s, Norfolk jackets became so popular that they were recommended for a range of activities, including bicycling, business, fishing, 'pleasuring', and 'the moorland'. The drab colours provided excellent camouflage for blood sports, and by 1897 they had outstripped the lounge jacket as the most stylish attire for cyclists. They were usually worn with matching knickerbockers, knitted stockings and a soft cap or hat.

Norfolk jackets were generally made of a hardwearing, woollen material such as Harris tweed and included large patch pockets and a belt of self-material. Individual coats varied in small design features according to individual tastes, type of activity or fashion. This example has simulated box pleats laid onto the foreparts and back, large flapped pockets attached to the hips, and breast pockets concealed under the front straps. It was probably worn for general country wear as inside one of the pockets are a piece of paper giving the monthly rainfall for the year 1900, a stamp, a metal pin and a piece of string.

Man's Norfolk jacket of tweed lined with sateen and striped cotton
and fastened with horn buttons. Machine-sewn and hand-finished.
British, 1890–1900
Given by Mr Martin Kamer
T.356-1984

On 3 June 1861 the sporting Earl Dunmore bought a 'fancy stripe flannel boating jacket' and a matching vest and trousers from Henry Poole & Co., the Savile Row tailor.[1] Similar styles were also worn for cricket and tennis and were popular seaside wear during the 1880s. They became so fashionable that *The Gentleman's Magazine* of 1884 remarked: 'Every man with a grain of respectability on the river puts on white trousers, with white flannel shirt, straw hat, striped flannel coat.' By the late nineteenth century gentlemen were wearing matching light-coloured suits, not only for sports, but also for relaxed holiday attire.

This suit is typical of the styles worn for boating in the 1890s. The jacket is constructed in the form of a 'three seamer', a slightly waisted coat with a central seam down the back and one on either side. Its three patch pockets have a distinctive line of stitching known as a swelled edge, a common feature of informal clothing styles. The trousers are cut wide and straight for ease of movement. Suits of this kind were also known as 'dittos' as the jacket, waistcoat and trousers are all made of the same material. This enhances the symmetry of the suit and focuses attention on details such as the elegant bone buttons and pin-striped flannel.

Attractive as these light colours were, they did show stains, and flannel had a tendency to shrink on washing. To prevent this *The Tailor and Cutter* of May 1888 suggested returning them to the tailor for cleaning or asking the laundress to scour them in cold water, adding oxalic acid to remove the dirt.

1. Fiona Anderson, *Henry Poole and Co. Savile Row Tailors 1861–1900* (London, 1998), p.91.

Man's boating suit of pin-striped flannel fastened with bone buttons.
British, 1890–96
Given by Dr C. W. Cunnington
T.113-1934

Clusters of flowers and leaf motifs enrich the sleeves and skirt of this charming dress. Embroidered in satin stitch, chain stitch and French knots, they are set in relief against a diaphanous ground of white muslin. The design trails down across the front of the dress and around the scalloped hemline to simulate a draped tunic-style garment slit up the side seam. This was a popular device and other fashionable worked borders included oak-leaf motifs, scrolling designs and tamboured snail patterns.

The front of the bodice is composed of a panel of bias-cut muslin, which is sewn onto the skirt rather like the bib of an apron so that it can be placed in position at the neck with pins. When the pins are removed the bib front falls away to reveal linen underflaps which fasten across the bust to give support.[1]

This type of bodice construction was very common and is known as the high stomacher front.

To ensure the front of the skirt hangs in a smooth, straight line, it is not gathered into the waistband. Drawstrings below the bust on either side of the bib allow the excess fabric to be held in neat folds under the arms and are fastened behind. The back of the skirt is gathered into the centre, helping to facilitate movement and produce the fashionable slightly rounded silhouette. Sometimes a small bustle pad was stitched inside at the waist to add to the effect.

1. These flaps sometimes fastened under the bust. See Janet Arnold, *Patterns of Fashion: Englishwomen's Dresses c.1660–1860* (London 1964/72), p.52.

Dress of muslin embroidered with wool. The bodice back and side fronts are lined with linen and there are linen undersleeves.
British, about 1808
Given by Messrs Harrods Ltd
T.684-1913

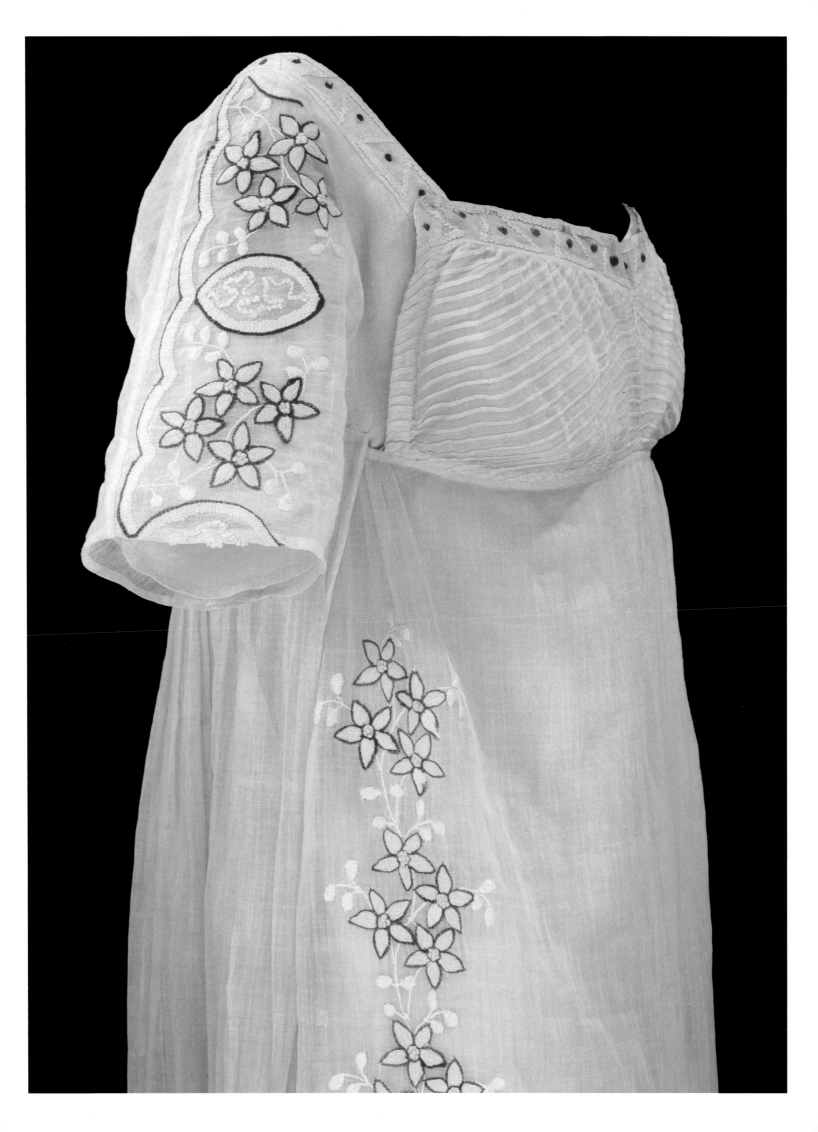

Attention to detail has been lavished on this bodice by Worth. The linings of 1890s gowns helped support the garments' silhouette and hold the outer fabric in a smooth line over the corset which would be worn underneath. Here, the foundation bodice is immaculately constructed to help create a perfect fit. Each piece of lining material has been cut to match the panels of outer fabric, and then both have been seamed together. To prevent the seam allowances from wrinkling they were notched at intervals, opened and then pressed flat. Whalebone supports were inserted into casings positioned on top of the seams.

The waist-tape anchored the bodice and helped define the waist. It was also the ideal position for the designer's name and the place where the garment was made, in this case C. Worth and Paris. By the late nineteenth century many couturiers and manufacturers were labelling their products, and the more glamorous the name and location, the better. The House of Worth started to identify its designs with labels in the early 1860s and introduced the woven signature label in the late 1880s. The allure of their garments was so strong that some labels were probably faked and placed in clothing of dubious quality.

For more information on this bodice see page 64.

Woman's bodice (internal back view) made of silk with grosgrain waist-tape and whalebone supports. Machine-sewn and hand-finished.
Charles Frederick Worth (1825–95) or Jean-Philippe Worth (1856–1926). Paris, 1890–93
Given by the Comtesse de Tremereuc and possibly worn by her mother
T.366-1960

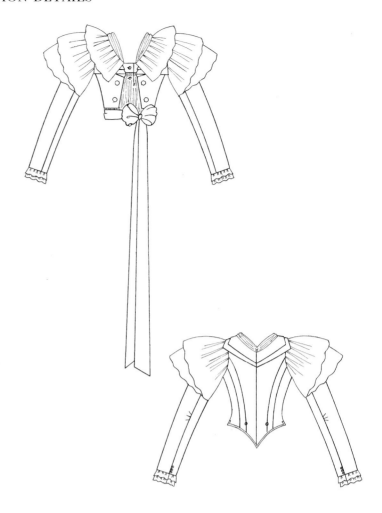

The line drawings depict an English dinner dress of about 1882. The dress is of rose pink satin trimmed with machine-embroidered net, the long bodice typical of the 1880s and fastened by lacing at the back. The skirt is of a tied-back style with a bustle decorated with a brocaded silk panel at the front and lace-edged satin flounces.

High-quality craftsmanship and meticulous attention to detail can clearly be seen by examining the inside construction of the bodice and noting the subtleties. It is fully lined in figured silk and hand-finished. Notches on seams and darts are gently rounded and give a pleasing appearance, and narrow strips of baleen (whalebone) are secured in the boning casings which are carefully sewn with minute stitches. The baleen stays in each casing are assembled in two sections with a break at the waist. The inside of the bodice is edged with rose coloured silk to give an elegant finish. The lace trimming at the neck, sleeves and hem secured on the inside of the bodice is sewn with stitches which could easily be unpicked to allow for removal and ease of laundering.

The use of the baleen allows for the corseted shaping and firm, long line of the bodice to be achieved and held to shape. The term 'whalebone' is commonly used, but baleen is not bone. It is a keratin material more closely allied to horn. It is found in the mouths of whales and some other cetaceans, where it is formed into elongated triangular plates used as food strainers. Each whale has between 260–360 of these plates along each side of the upper jaw. Baleen varies in colour from black to cream, and the baleen plates of the Bowhead whale (*Balaena mysticetus*) can measure up to 4.5 metres in length.
M. K.

Dinner dress (internal front view of bodice) made of satin trimmed with machine-embroidered net, lined with silk and narrow strips of baleen (whalebone).
British, about 1882
Given by Mrs Theresa Horner
T.130-1958

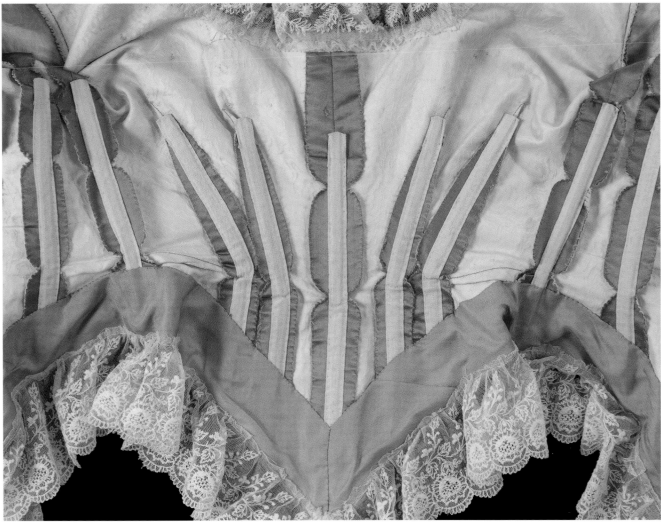

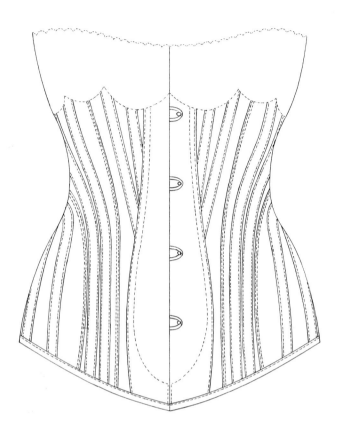

Technological developments had a huge impact on the manufacture of corsets during the second half of the nineteenth century. The introduction of the sewing machine into corset-making during the 1850s was one of the major improvements, as it speeded up production and reduced costs.

This machine-sewn corset is made from ten shaped pieces of red sateen, which are seamed together. Vertical strips of tan leather delineate the position of the whalebone supports and busk which provide the solid foundation structure underneath. The regularity of the stitches along the strips of leather illustrates the power of the sewing machine that could stitch neatly through this durable material. Their evenness, combined with the sturdiness of leather, reinforces the casings into which the whalebone strips are inserted. Whalebone was popular as it was strong yet light and flexible, moulding the body into the desired shape without easily snapping. An alternative to whalebone was cording, whereby a twisted cord made from hemp, cotton or paper was inserted between two layers of fabric and sewn on either side to keep it in place.

The corset is laced at the back through metal eyelet holes which were first patented by Thomas Rogers in March 1823.[1] They proved much stronger than eyelets bound with silk or cotton thread and had a smoother inner surface which assisted with lacing. In front, the corset is fastened with a two-part busk and metal fastenings. This style of closure enabled the wearer to put on or remove her corset without help and was widely used throughout the corset-making industry. It was the result of many earlier experiments, including busks which could be separated by pulling a catch, and metal blades fitted with springs so that the fastenings simultaneously detached. In 1848 Joseph Cooper patented the slot-and-stud style fastening[2] seen in this example, whereby a stud on one side of the split-busk slotted into a keyhole-shaped plate on the other. The design worked so well that it became the standard type of metal corset fastening and is still used today.

For more information on this corset see page 144.

1. Patent no. 4766, 1823 (British Library)
2. Patent no. 12,318, 1848 (British Library)

Corset, 'Brown's Patent Dermathistic No. 2076'. Made of sateen lined with coutil.
The bone channels, busk and centre back steels are covered in leather.
British, 1883–95
T.84-1980

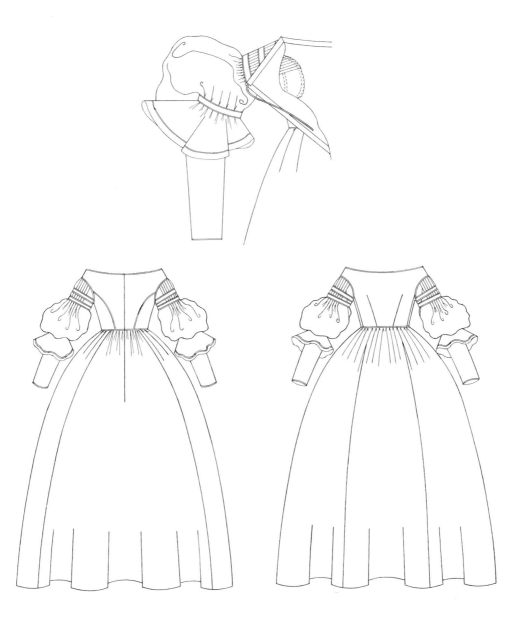

Puffed, pleated and frilled sleeves fall from the shoulders of this striking day dress. Although sleeves had diminished in size by 1836, eye-catching designs compensated for their lack of fullness. Fashion magazines closely monitored the changing styles, and in March 1836 *Townsend's Monthly Selection of Parisian Costumes* reported:

The war of extermination which has been raging these two months between BOUFFANT SLEEVES and TIGHT SLEEVES has not ceased … The extremely wide sleeves are inconvenient and ridiculous, whilst the close sleeves … are prejudicial to the shoulders by contracting them. The wisest plan therefore is to adopt all that is really useful of each, giving to the tight sleeves the ornaments which usually belong to the bouffant sleeves … ruches, garnitures, ruffles, manchettes or bows; in fact all that can give them variety and novelty.

This pair of sleeves has been altered to update the dress to the latest fashions. They were originally constructed in the 'gigot' or 'leg of mutton' style fashionable from about 1825–35. The 'gigot' was very full at the top, tapering to a narrow circumference at the wrist and was usually constructed in one piece. To adapt them the dressmaker has inserted pleats below the shoulder to contain the fullness and has confined the folds with bands of self-fabric. Pleating was popular as it emphasized the drooping shoulder line, and here the lining is pleated onto the outer fabric for reinforcement, adding to the effect. A wider band of fabric helps to hold the puff in place above the elbow and the frill gives the impression of an oversleeve.

The low, rounded neckline, almost slipping off the shoulders, is typical of fashions for this date. Its simple shape complements the lines of the bodice and skirt which is pleated at the waist so that it falls in elegant folds to the hem. Decoration is provided by the fabric printed in a striking design of shamrocks and flowers on a chequered ground. The rich red and shades of brown suggest the colour of falling leaves, the time of year when warm woollen dresses like this one would have been ideal.

Day dress of wool printed with a design of clover leaves. Lined with cotton and glazed cotton.
British, 1836–38
Given by Mrs H. M. Shepherd
T.11-1935

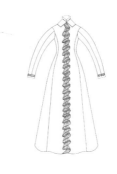

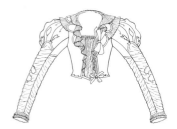

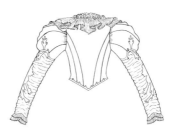

Maroon and yellow pleated frills cascade down the front of this dress, concealing the button fastenings. The frills are composed of two narrow lengths of silk, which have been knife-pleated and then twisted backwards and forwards. This type of trimming was highly fashionable during the 1870s, and pleated flounces also formed elaborate decoration on the front, back, hems and trains of skirts. Creating such regular pleats by hand would have been very time-consuming, and contemporary fashion magazines are full of advertisements for 'Kilting Machines', otherwise known as pleating machines. Manufacturers promised that these machines could kilt (knife-pleat) any fabric by steam, from the lightest silk to the heaviest serge, with excellent and long-lasting results.

Woman's dress of silk trimmed with silk. Machine-sewn and hand-finished.
British, 1877–79
Given by Mrs M. Garland
T.414-1996

Fine chiffon pleats resembling the inside cap of a mushroom are draped across the front of this bodice. They were created through a heat-setting process and are reminiscent of the pleats that Mariano Fortuny later patented for his Delphos dresses in 1909. Here, the pleats are caught onto a boned bodice foundation to imitate a blouse and conceal the front dress fastening. They are framed on either side by dainty frills of chiffon. Thin, transparent materials, delicate ruffles, falls of lace and pouched false fronts were a fashionable feature of late 1890s dress, showing how trends were moving towards a softer, lighter look. This ensemble displays an elaborate melange of fabric, embroidery and trimmings, including pleated chiffon, brown silk velvet, sequins embroidered onto silver stems, lime green taffeta and applied velvet slipper orchids.

Woman's bodice of silk chiffon and ribbed silk with applied hand-painted velvet flowers.
Nicaud & Cie. Paris, about 1897
Given by Sir Herbert Ingram Bart., Captain B. Ingram MC, and Captain Collingwood Ingram
T.206-1927

Pleated bodices and gathered skirts were highly fashionable during the 1840s. Bodices like this one were constructed with extra fullness in front that was arranged into converging pleats. These pleats were stitched into position on a lining from just below the bust to the waist, a process that demanded neat sewing as the stitches were visible. The resulting fan-like folds helped to suggest a rounded bosom above a narrow waist. Here, the effect is emphasized by the striped fabric following the line of the pleats.

Skirts were cut from several widths of unshaped material that were tightly gathered into the waistband by a method known as 'cartridge' or 'organ' pleating. These were small tubular pleats closely drawn together to create a dome-shaped silhouette when worn over stiffened petticoats. In this example a narrow band of bias-cut piping delineates the waistline and separates the two different styles of pleating.

Day dress of shot silk with an integrated ribbon stripe fastened in front with wooden buttons covered in silk and at the back with hooks and eyes. Hand-sewn and lined with cotton and whalebone strips.
British, 1848–50
Given by John Joshua Sprigge, Esq.
T.190-1917

Pleated folds descend from the shoulder seam to the waistband of this bodice, forming a crossover front. They are secured in place with decorative rows of orange chain stitch and the waist is fastened with a single hook and eye closure. This creates an attractive V-shaped opening, which would be filled with a chemisette or soft collar for modesty. The pleats on the skirt echo those on the bodice and also help distribute its fullness. By this date skirts were so wide that they were often worn over whalebone hoops or a horsehair petticoat for support.

Similar garments adorned the pages of fashion magazines and were praised for their stylish construction and graceful simplicity. They were considered ideal for the promenade or morning visits, particularly when made of plain silk. This dress survived, along with a large collection of historical costume belonging to one family, due to a descendant's interest in amateur dramatics.

Day dress of silk lined with linen and glazed cotton.
British, 1838–40
T.51-2002

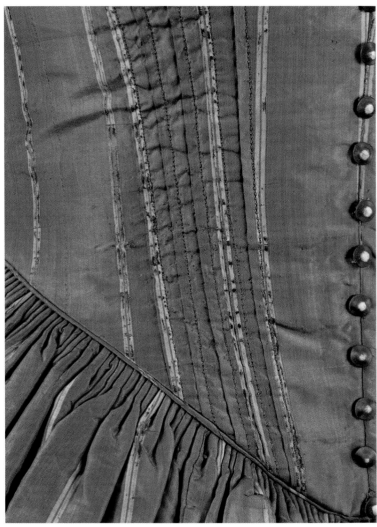

Green chenille pom-poms enhance this charming spencer and matching dress. These are attached to a continuous silk cord and stitched into place around the collar, cuffs and down the front of the bodice. Their position on each side of the front fastening evokes the buttons and buttonholes on a man's coat. Around the sash and hem of the skirt they hang freely, following the movements of the wearer.

Spencers were ideal for summer as they could be worn over a light dress out of doors. They were cut on similar lines to the high-waisted bodice of the gown, and the material and trimmings often matched. In this example the spencer opens to reveal a shirred bodice decorated with two pom-poms and delicate embroidered net sleeves. Corresponding accessories completed the look, and Elizabeth Grant expresses her delight when she is seventeen and gains a new wardrobe complete with a bonnet adorned with 'blush roses' and a 'new spencer … of blush-rose pink'.[1]

1. Elizabeth Grant, *Memoirs of a Highland Lady 1797–1827* (Edinburgh, 1988), Vol.1, p.328.

Spencer and dress made of taffeta trimmed with chenille and silk cord. Lined with cotton.
British, 1807–10
Given by Mrs E. Sanford
T.60-1962

A cascade of trimming adorns this woman's day outfit, reflecting the passion for passementerie decoration such as fringe, braid, gimp, ribbon, tassels and cord. Some of the most fashionable garments combined passementerie with applied bands of velvet, complementing the colour of the dress and adding rich textures. The fringe on this bodice is composed of strands of black hand-knotted silk forming openings into which 'poms' of brown chenille are inserted to create the tufted look. Identical fringed trimmings are also applied to the skirt flounces, and they must have swayed with the movements of the wearer, creating rippled effects.

Passementerie dress trimmings were similar to those used on beds, windows and upholstery, and a fashionable woman must have looked very much at home when surrounded by tasselled valances and padded chairs embellished with fringe. Such luxurious upholstery trimmings were essential elements of nineteenth-century style, helping to add the required luxury to rooms in the form of colour and texture. They had the same effect on fashion and became particularly popular from the 1850s onwards. French manufacturers led the field in innovative techniques and imaginative trimmings, while the British followed their styles, adapting them for their own market.

Promenade dress (bodice and skirt) of silk trimmed with silk and chenille passementerie.
Bodice lined with silk and whalebone strips.
British or French, 1855–57
Given by Mme Tussauds
T.325-1977

Luxurious velvet dresses embellished with fringe trimmings were highly fashionable during the 1850s. Their virtues did not escape the attention of the press, and in September 1857 *The Illustrated London News* announced:

Fringe was never so greatly in demand as at the present time … Fringe may be said to be the most becoming of all trimmings for a lady's dress; it seems to possess the power of imparting lightness and suppleness to the movements of the wearer. When we see a lady whose skirt, corsage, sleeves &c. are trimmed with wavy silken fringe, its graceful effect is sufficiently obvious.

To enhance the effect, small, silk-covered balls, tassels, pearls and beads were often suspended amidst the fringe, resembling passementerie found on upholstery. The idea was immortalized in the film *Gone with the Wind* (1949) when Scarlett O'Hara tries to win over the affections of Rhett Butler in an attempt to save her beloved home, Tara. Desperate for something attractive to wear, she tears down a set of 'moss-green velvet curtains'[1] and has them made up into a striking dress complete with a heavy fringe and cord tassels.

When applied in rows, fringes also simulated flounces and made the skirts look even wider. In this example, the bodice is made with a basque, which was a separate extension below the waist, flaring out over the hips. This type of construction was popular and often gave the impression of a flounce at the top of the skirt, particularly when trimmed with velvet or fringe. The skirt is composed of two layers, with the top tier extending from the waistband as far as the fifth row of fringe and the bottom attached to a taffeta underskirt. This accentuates the flounced effect of the fringe and helps distribute the weight of the heavy skirt over the dome-shaped crinoline cage which would have been worn underneath.

For more information about this outfit see page 112.

1. Margaret Mitchell, *Gone with the Wind* (Great Britain, first published 1936), p.531. NB: there is no mention of passementerie trimmings in the book.

Promenade dress (bodice and skirt) made of silk plush and trimmed with
silk fringe headed with braid. Bodice lined with silk and whalebone strips.
British, 1855–57
Given by Mme Tussauds
T.324-1977

Skirts reached some of their most exaggerated proportions during the early 1860s. They tended to be flatter in front than the rounded shapes of the 1850s, and fanned out behind creating an enormous expanse of fabric and a wide circumference at the hem. Skirts of this dimension were often worn over 'cage' petticoats made of steel hoops to give them their distinctive shape. The ever-increasing width made the waist look smaller, and this effect was accentuated by Swiss belts, a type of waistband pointed above and below. The belt in this example has long pointed 'lappets' stiffened with whalebone to create a smooth line over the hips.

A variety of patterned fabrics and trimmings added to the dramatic impact of these styles. This fashionable evening dress is ornamented with applied velvet bands and loops, creating a castellated effect on the bodice and base of the skirt. A delicate lace edging emphasizes the low neckline, while the fabric stripes slant inwards towards the waist and outwards over the petticoat,

following the contours of the silhouette. The 'lappets' adorning the shoulders and Swiss belt are trimmed with tassels composed of silk fringe and wooden balls covered in interlocking gimp (silk wrapped around a cotton core). They resemble designs for lambrequins which were used as pelmets or as decoration for mantelpieces, revealing how the taste for passementerie also captured the dress designer's imagination. *The Illustrated London News* of February 1861 commented on the popularity of such ornamental trimmings and warned against the expense:

Passementerie is more than ever in vogue, especially for the ornamentation of silk dresses; but it is of a high price, on account of the peculiar requirements of its composition. It is no longer a simple trimming for corsages and skirts, but has to be manufactured in accordance with the exigencies of the mode, which demands peculiar forms and series of ornaments; hence the inevitable increase in its cost.

Evening dress (bodice, skirt and Swiss belt) of moiré woven with vertical stripes and trimmed with velvet, hand-made bobbin lace, silk fringe and tassels. Bodice and Swiss belt lined with silk and whalebone strips.
British, 1861–63
Given by Lady Elizabeth McIntosh
T.115-1979

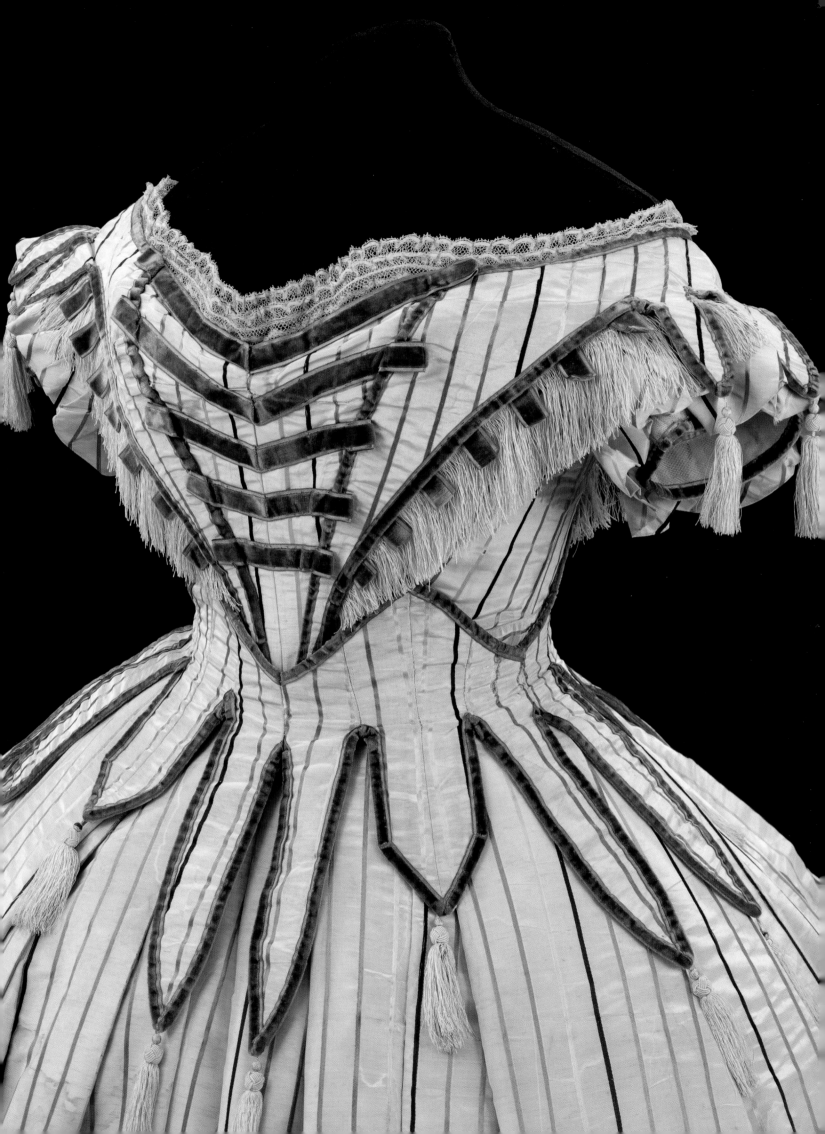

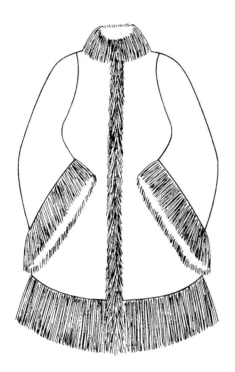

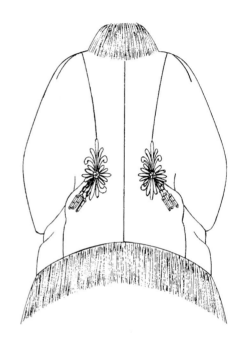

Ornate, elongated trimmings positioned on the back of this dolman accentuate its bustled silhouette and complement the fabric pattern. Rich passementerie such as tassels, rosettes, braid, cord, tufts and fringe frequently embellished women's fashionable dress, creating luxurious effects. They resembled the trimmings found on curtains, cushions and upholstery and were made using similar techniques and materials which frequently resulted in hours of highly skilled work.

The passementerie illustrated here is composed of three wooden steeple-shaped moulds wrapped in blue floss silk. This produces a vibrant sheen and a perfect surface for the multi-coloured cord that is attached vertically and horizontally through processes known as striping and plaiting. This was done by hand, probably specifically for this garment as they harmonize with the colours, enriching its overall exotic effect. The moulds are suspended from a rosette by knotted cord attachments so that they would sway in a beguiling manner when the wearer moved. To complete the design, curving leaf forms composed of lengths of applied cord echo the swirling shapes of the fabric pattern.

For more information on this mantle see page 102.

Woman's dolman of woven wool trimmed with passementerie and lined with quilted silk-satin.
Woven in India for the European market, 1878–82
Given by T. R. H. The Duke and Duchess of Gloucester
T.44-1957

The Natural World

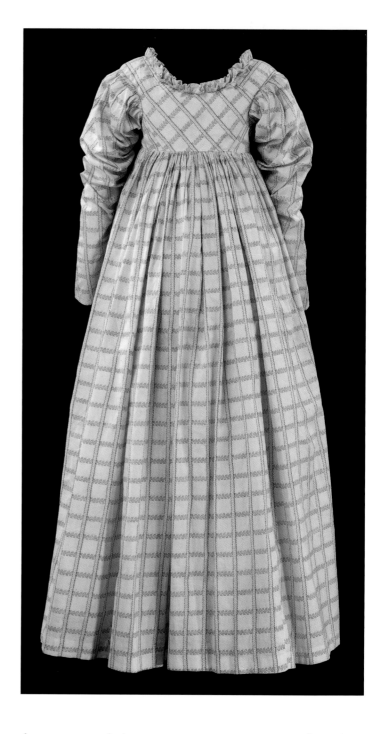

Thorny stems and leafy bands intersect on this dress, producing a trellis-like effect. They give the cotton a light and delicate appearance, which is heightened by the double neck frill and gathered sleeves. Similar garments are depicted in fashion plates of the time and in portraits by artists, particularly the works of Jean-Auguste-Dominique Ingres (1780–1867). In his drawing *Rosina Meli, Madame Guillon Lethière, and her daughter Letizia*, Rosina's checked dress closely resembles the one in this example, except that she also wears a fashionable ruff.[1]

The back of the bodice has been shortened to correspond with the fashion for high waistlines. It may also indicate that this dress was worn during pregnancy, as garments were often adapted for this period in a woman's life. Contrary to popular myth, many women remained socially active right up to the time of their delivery. High-waisted dresses like this one provided comfortable and convenient maternity wear, which also concealed early physical changes. The drawstrings at the top and bottom of the front flaps may also have been inserted for pregnancy, to accommodate a growing bust size.

1. See Aileen Ribiero, *Ingres in Fashion* (New Haven & London, 1999), p.53.

Day dress (back view) of printed cotton with cotton bodice lining and under flaps.
British, about 1814
Given by Messrs Harrods Ltd
T.674-1913

Three-dimensional floral decoration is used to great effect on the hem of this evening or ball dress of 1815. It is constructed on a ground of white net, the entire surface of which is covered with yellow satin stitches applied over blue satin-stitched half-moon shapes. The lower skirt is trimmed with a flounce of plain machine-made net headed and edged with blue satin trim and richly embroidered with a repeated trailing design of blue and gold flowers. Blue satin-edged lobes of net also trim the lower skirt. The bodice is decorated with blue satin bands and a cream ribbon finishes the waist.

The flowers, worked to match the blue satin trim, are taken from a design of moss roses and rosebuds and created by means of embroidery and the application of three-dimensional petal shapes made in blue satin and cream crêpe. The leaf motifs and straggling stalks linking the flower sprays around the hemline are worked in silk chenille in golden yellow and brown.

On 18 June 1815 Napoleon Bonaparte (1769–1821) was defeated at the Battle of Waterloo. A dress of this type would have been a suitable choice for a well-dressed lady attending the balls or parties held to celebrate this event.
M. K.

Evening or ball dress of machine-made silk bobbin
net decorated with hand-embroidered and applied flowers.
British, about 1815
T.279-1973

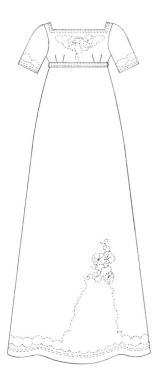
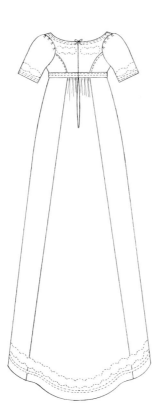

This evening dress has the typical high-waisted and fashionable line of 1806–08. It is gathered at the back from the high waist-line and is very slightly trained to give an elegant silhouette (see line drawing). The bodice, sleeves and hem are decorated with a sumptuous decoration of trailing nasturtiums. The flowers, leaves and tendrils are worked in fairly naturalistic colours and simple stitches, but are enriched in appearance by the use of silk chenille to give a soft velvety texture which adds richness to the otherwise unsophisticated embroidery.

The nasturtium is a simple, rather dull choice of flower for evening wear, but perhaps the choice was purposeful and pointed. In the language of flowers, different blooms convey hidden meanings, the intricacies of which have largely fallen into disuse today but may have been understood by middle and upper class young women at this time. The traditional meaning and symbolism of the nasturtium was 'patriotism'. Viewed within the context of contemporary history, immediately after the victory of Horatio Nelson at Trafalgar (1805), and in the period of the Napoleonic Wars (1793–1815), it is perhaps a subtle reference to the strong nationalistic feelings at the time and a statement by the wearer whose family members may have been fighting for their country.
M. K.

Evening dress of crêpe embroidered with nasturtium flowers, leaves and tendrils worked in silk chenille.
British, 1806–08
T.241-1983

The wild strawberries printed onto this dress look good enough to eat! An undulating motif based on bamboo, pinks and anemones add to the effect, evoking the hues and smells of a country garden. Even the colours listed in contemporary fashion magazines have floral names such as 'sweet-scented pea', 'primrose', 'geranium' and 'pale rose'.

A fascination with printed flowers was nothing new in textile design, but it received a new impetus during the 1830s. Technical improvements in printing coupled with advances in dye chemistry during the early nineteenth century meant that floral prints could now be mass-produced at low prices. The repeal of the excise duty on printed textiles in 1831 also went a long way to reduce costs. As demand and output grew, the range of printed designs multiplied. Manufacturers constantly had to respond to the requirements of women's fashion for increasingly elaborate floral patterns, particularly on day wear, and a profusion of flowers and foliage graced women's dresses, including roses, hyacinths, sweet peas and creepers.

Inspiration came from a variety of sources, including botanical engravings, pattern books and plants grown in gardens or conservatories. Some printed fabrics were even criticized for being too close to nature.

Day dress of challis printed with flowers and lined with glazed cotton and linen.
British, 1837–40
Given by Miss E. Tucker and part of the trousseau of Sarah Elizabeth Bruce (b. 1805) but never worn
T.184-1931

The irises, red turks-cap lilies and red salvias on this dress are so finely executed that they are reminiscent of botanical illustrations. They reveal the skill of the pattern-drawer who designed the fabric pattern and often specified the printing colours. From the late eighteenth century developments in dye technology meant that the pattern-drawer needed to be as much chemist as designer to understand these new and complicated processes.

Once the blocks were cut, it was the printer's job to transfer the designs and colours onto the fabric. If a block did not register[1] correctly it could create shadow effects or exposed areas of white, which were particularly noticeable on a pale ground. The blue flowers on this example have been painted or 'pencilled' onto the cotton, a technique developed to minimize problems with oxidization when printing indigo dyes. Faint yellow and cream stripes blending into one another shows that this fabric has also been printed in the 'rainbow style'.[2]

1. The term 'register' means to establish the correct position of the block on the cloth.
2. 'Rainbow style' was a method of block-printing invented by the paper-stainer Spoerlin of Vienna.

Day dress (sleeve detail) of block-printed cotton, part-lined with linen.
British, about 1828
Given by Mrs H. K. Ludgate
T.151-1968

Country and garden flowers were a popular design source, emphasizing the sense of romance that flourished in 1830s fashion. Some flowers were drawn directly from nature, others copied from botanical illustrations or pattern books and many were the fanciful creations of the pattern-drawer. The heather depicted on this dress, with its narrow, spiky stem and small pink tubular flowers, looks as if it has sprung directly from the moorland or wayside. The yellow and blue flowers are marigolds and asters, and valerian on leafy stalks completes the staggered block-printed repeat.

The bold floral design is set against a striking red ground. This vivid dye was based on madder and became known as Turkey or Adrianople red. A popular colour in the nineteenth century, it proved ideal for handkerchiefs, scarf borders and petticoats when printed with fanciful designs. The colour intensity gives a luminous quality to the flowers printed on this dress and the wearer would definitely have stood out in the crowd. The pattern was intended for overall impact rather than close scrutiny, as the block-print has not registered, in places creating shadow effects on the leaves and petals. The vibrant design also conceals a loose panel at the front of the bodice that could be unfastened at the waist and raised for nursing.

Day dress (sleeve detail) of block-printed cotton, lined with cotton.
British, 1825–30
Given by Miss D. A. Frearson
T.74-1988

Curling tendrils separated by undulating lines and a latticework of simulated trimming adorn this printed day dress. They are reminiscent of the naturalistic textile designs by late eighteenth- and early nineteenth-century pattern-drawers. William Kilburn (1745–1818) was one of the most eminent designers and his fragile flowers, offset by skeletal leaves, fern roots, delicate seaweed and coral-like forms, inspired many later textiles. *Trompe l'oeil* effects were also popular from 1820–50, and in this example the sinuous lines edged with green imitate applied braid.

The stylized textile design and gentle colours enhance the dress, following the curves of the bodice and the gathered folds of the wide skirt. Bias-cut strips of fabric decorate the bell-shaped ends of the sleeves and a pleated panel descends from the shoulder to the centre front of the bodice. Many dresses of this date were decorated with trimmings of self-fabric, focusing the eye on the fabric pattern or richness of the material as well as the fashionable silhouette. This garment would have been worn over a corset and several stiff petticoats to give the skirt its dome-like shape.

Day dress of roller-printed wool, part-lined with cotton and whalebone strips.
British, 1848–50
Given by Messrs Harrods Ltd
T.797-1913

This richly patterned velvet waistcoat would have complemented the darker colours of a coat. The dense design of roses and forget-me-nots changes colour according to the light, sometimes emerald on a grey ground, at other times tinged with blue. Waistcoats tended to be one of the more elaborate and colourful components of the male wardrobe, which is partly why they survive in relatively large numbers. They might have been kept for their decorative quality or for sentimental reasons when they went out of fashion.

Different styles of waistcoat were worn according to the cut of the coat, season, time of day and occasion. They could be single- or double-breasted and were often made of velvet for winter wear and light silks for the summer. Particularly flamboyant examples caused comment, such as the brightly coloured, embroidered waistcoats worn by Charles Dickens on his American tour in 1842, which were labelled by the press as 'somewhat in the flash order'.[1]

1. See Penelope Byrde, *The Male Image* (London, 1979), p.86.

Man's waistcoat of voided silk velvet, backed with glazed cotton and lined with cotton.
Probably French, 1845–50
Given by Miss Kathleen S. Lyon
T. 96-1935

This is a striking and elaborately patterned waistcoat woven with a delicate pattern of peacock feathers and naturalistic pendulous flower forms based on honeysuckle and hazel twigs. These are picked out in accents of blue, cream and fawn.

The waistcoat has a curved roll collar and fits neatly to just below the waist, dating it in style to 1845 to 1850. The six buttons are hand-made and constructed over a wooden core. They fasten at the lower front. The pockets on each forepart, the lapels and the bottom edges of the waistcoat are finished with a fine braid. The back is of deep red silk and it is lined with cream glazed cotton.

Peacock feathers were a popular motif for fabrics worn by both men and women in the middle and later part of the nineteenth century. In some instances interpreted as symbolic of vanity and luxury, the peacock also represented gracious or knightly demeanour in medieval times, the resurrection and eternal life and the beauty of an eternity to come in heaven.
M. K.

Man's waistcoat of jacquard-woven silk with a pattern of peacock feathers.
British, 1845–50
Given by Mr H. Arnold Ovenden
T.1-1954

This gentleman's waistcoat is sprinkled with a dainty design of roses and branching stems floating against an oyster silk ground. The pattern evokes eighteenth-century Spitalfields silks, but is woven using a jacquard loom invented in 1801 by Joseph-Marie Charles Jacquard (1752–1834). Jacquard-weaving came into general use in Britain during the 1830s, saving time and money as it allowed complex patterns to be woven automatically rather than by the labour-intensive techniques of the hand-operated drawloom. Although ideally suited to large elaborate patterns, it was also used for the delicate designs which adorned many fashionable garments during the 1840s and 1850s. The colours and floral motifs scattered over this waistcoat are very similar to those found on stylish women's dresses of the period.

A man's waistcoat of jacquard-woven silk fastened with detachable metal buttons. Backed and lined with cotton.
British, about 1850
Given by Miss W. A. Skeggs
T.82-1954

Waistcoats were a prominent feature of men's dress as the coat was often worn unbuttoned. Floral and foliate designs in harmonious colourways were fashionable in the 1840s and 1850s, although many also favoured bright tartans and loud checks. In this example, a delicate pattern of vine leaves sprinkled with speedwell (veronica) is jacquard-woven in blue and cream giving a variety of textural effects. The repeat is carefully matched on the lapels and foreparts and needlewoven[1] button coverings blend in with the colours.

Double-breasted styles like this one with buttoned-back lapels became popular in about 1853 for morning or walking attire. The waistcoat can also be dated by the base of the foreparts which are lined with leather, a feature that only appeared from 1845–55. A japanned buckle stamped with 1853 also suggests a precise date, although it could have been in the tailor's stock for years before it was used.

1. Needleweaving is a technique often used in passementerie whereby threads often in contrasting colours are passed in and out of threads laid down vertically.

Waistcoat of jacquard-woven silk, lined with cotton and backed with scrim.
British, about 1853
Given by Miss W. Shaw
T.10-1951

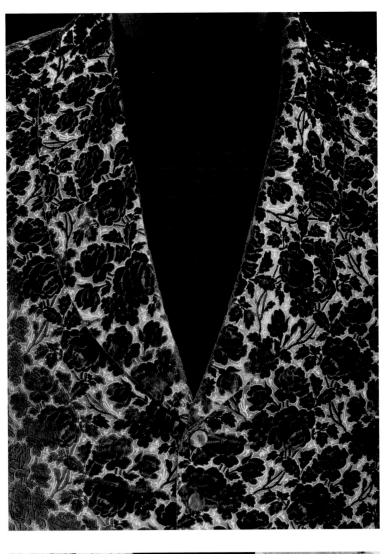

This elegant bustle dress displays a dense pattern of violets spring-ing from a bed of vine leaves. The design would have been woven by a powered jacquard loom and is an example of a good com-mercially produced fabric. Jacquard was a system of weaving elaborate patterns invented in 1801 by Joseph-Marie Jacquard (1752–1834) that came into general use in Britain during the 1830s. The jacquard loom used a series of perforated cards to reg-ulate which warp threads were lifted and which were lowered to form the design. The mechanism replaced the labour-intensive drawloom, producing a versatile, quicker and cheaper method of weaving. Costs were cut further by the use of power to activate the looms which meant that one weaver could oversee a large number of looms, increasing production while dramatically reduc-ing the number of workers. By the middle of the nineteenth century, large weaving factories were being developed throughout

the north of England, and Macclesfield was associated with the production of patterned silk dress fabrics like this one.

The floral design complements the construction of this dress, accentuating the closely fitted lines of the bodice and drapery on the front of the skirt. It also flows in sweeping folds over the bus-tle, which by the mid-1880s jutted out almost at right angles from behind. Bustles were often a separate structure attached around the waist and included crinolettes made of steel half-hoops, down-filled pads and wire mesh structures. By 1885 the bustle was often incorporated into the back of the foundation skirt itself in the form of a small pad attached to the waistband and horizontal rows of steel which could be pulled into a curved shape. This dress has a foundation skirt of grey denim that is cut straight in front and gathered and pleated at the back to follow the lines of the separate bustle worn underneath.

Day dress (bodice and skirt) of jacquard-woven silk fastened with mother-of-pearl buttons and
trimmed with dark blue silk decorated with honey-combing. Bodice lined with cotton and whalebone strips.
British, about 1885
Given by the Revd W. H. Padget
Circ.204-1958

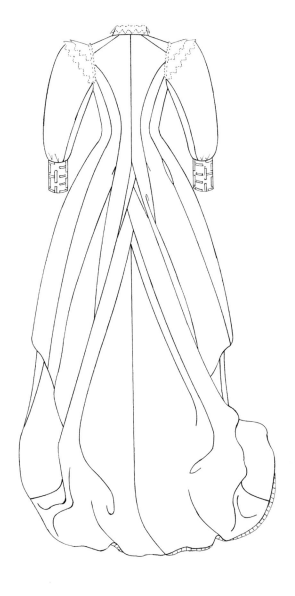

Clusters of oranges against a dramatic black ground produce a kaleidoscope effect on the back of this woman's dress. Parts of the fruits disappear into a seam or pleat but are cleverly matched on each side of the garment to retain the symmetry. The textured appearance of the peel is so lifelike that one can almost touch, taste and smell the oranges. This realistic pattern was created using sensitive colour combinations and a highly sophisticated jacquard-weaving technique and was probably executed by Spitalfields silk manufacturers in London.

The fabric also shows the influence of Oriental, and particularly Japanese decorative styles. A taste for Japanese art and design was stimulated by the International Exhibition of 1862 (London), during which many people saw the country's wares for the first time. Textile designers did much to promote and assimilate elements of Japanese style into patterns for dress and furnishing fabrics. Clarity of form and colour with unbroken outlines were some of the main characteristics derived from Japan, and black backgrounds were also very popular. The contrasting colours and clearly defined motifs in this example are typical of this style, although the actual dress construction conforms to the fashionable Western silhouette.

Dinner dress made of jacquard-woven silk trimmed in front
with silk ribbon and black machine lace. Bodice supported with whalebone strips.
British, about 1891
Given by Sir Herbert Ingram Bart., Captain B. S. Ingram MC, and Captain Collingwood Ingram
T.201-1927

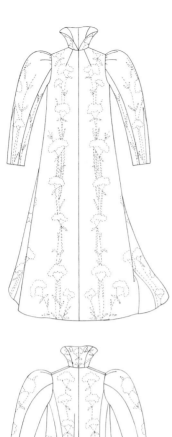

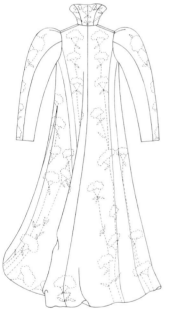

Slender stems of cow parsley stand out against rich velvet, conjuring up images of country hedgerows and a midnight sky. Each flower head is composed of four felt petals applied with a French knot, and the stalks and leaves are embroidered in feather stitch and couching. They are skilfully made and true to nature in both colour and design, unlike many of the stylized patterns on fashionable dress fabrics at this time.

Wild flowers were a popular decorative motif for the Arts and Crafts movement in dress as they evoked the return to 'Simple Life' styles from the mid-1880s onwards. These styles were based on an imaginary rural simplicity, returning to cottage industry, handcrafted techniques and countryside flowers. Embroiderers following the 'Simple Life' tended to use plain grounds scattered with delicate floral motifs. Appliqué was also popular as it was quick and enabled the needleworker to capture the essence of a plant very swiftly.

The cow parsley design on this evening coat closely resembles Arts and Crafts models in subject, design and execution. The construction of the garment, however, conforms to highly fashionable evening wear with its close-fitting bodice, long sweeping skirts and high 'Medici' collar supported with wire. It was possibly made in a couture house and then embroidered later according to the wearer's taste. Very few women were courageous enough to wear the simple dresses favoured by Arts and Crafts protagonists, but they might have adapted fashionable styles to show their artistic leanings.

Evening coat, silk velvet decorated with silk and appliqué embroidery and insertions of knotted cotton thread. Lined with silk.
Probably British, about 1900
Given by Mrs A. Poliakoff
T.49-1962

The widespread enthusiasm and fascination for naturalia in the nineteenth century resulted in an extensive use of natural and animal products for dress and accessories. Straw is surprisingly versatile and makes a very attractive and extraordinary decoration. This small semi-circular veil of black machine-made net would have been a charming trimming for a straw bonnet of the period. The veil is sprinkled with petite flower heads of stamped-out straw, each with a black glass bead in the centre. However, it is the three-dimensional bees that highlight the decoration. Three of the bees are evenly placed on the black open-work machine-made lace border, and one slightly off-centre on the veil. They are made of straw veneer and straw thread, black silk thread and glass beads. All straw motifs were probably made in Switzerland, but the veil was most likely assembled in France. France was the leading manufacturer of straw-decorated objects until the mid-nineteenth century.
H. P.

Veil of machine-made net with straw decoration.
French, 1860s
T.772-1972

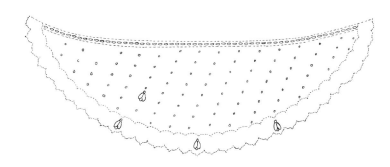

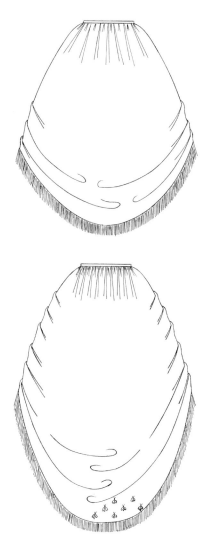

Charming and simple motifs of embroidered ladybirds in flight decorate this white machine-made net overskirt. It is short in front and looped up at the sides, then long at the back to form a train. The ladybirds are worked in red floss silk and black chenille and each is decorated with an iridescent grain-shaped glass bead which adds a little sparkle to an otherwise plain, unsophisticated motif. The hem of the overskirt is trimmed with a white silk fringe.

Nearly all cultures believe that the ladybird is lucky, and the Victorians believed that if a ladybird alighted on your hand, you would be receiving new gloves; if it landed on your head, then a new hat; and so forth. Its function as a species that would feed on aphids and scale insect pests was well known long before the nineteenth century to both gardeners and commercial growers alike. Ladybirds abounded in hop fields, which were an important commercial crop, and their beneficial actions would have been noticed long before scientific records gave account of them in print in 1861.
M. K.

Overskirt of machine-made net decorated with ladybirds.
British, about 1870
Given by Miss Alice A. Little
T.102-1922

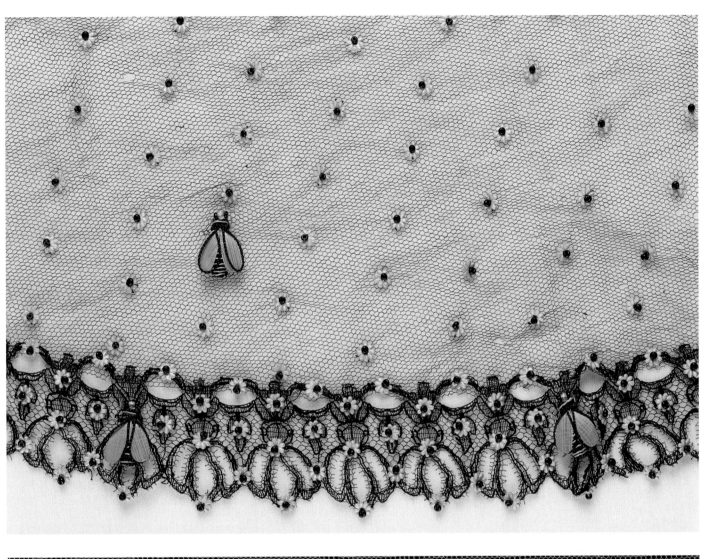

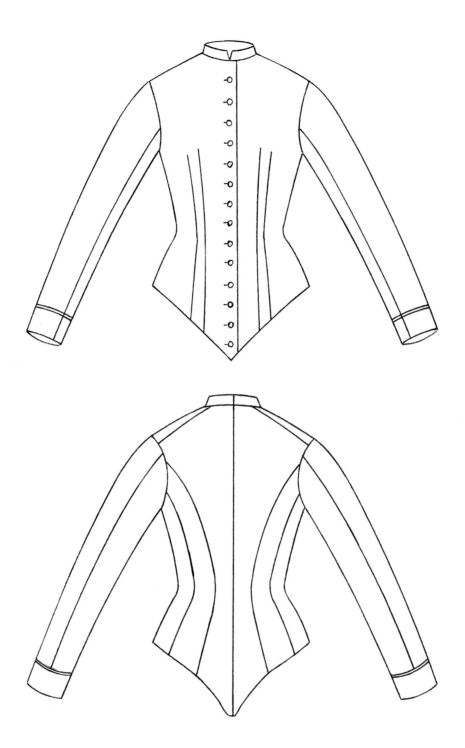

An exuberant design of birds and moths embroidered onto midnight blue silk velvet adorns this late nineteenth-century jacket. The jacket has been cut out and made up and the embroidery applied after construction. Floss silk has been used to work the embroidery in long and short stitches and satin stitch, but the work is crudely executed and may have been domestic work undertaken at home rather than by a professional seamstress. The velvet may have been reused from an earlier garment as there are small joins under the arms indicating that there was not quite sufficient velvet to cut the panels out in one piece. The jacket, boned with baleen, has fitted sleeves, a tightly nipped-in waist, and long pointed front and back typical of the late 1870s–early 1880s style.

Dating from a period when there was a strong interest and focus on the natural world, and frequent expeditions by plant hunters and explorers seeking new discoveries of nature, it is perhaps interesting that the species of birds and insects chosen to decorate this garment are fanciful and stylized and not drawn from life or images of known species. The bird and insect motifs may have been taken from an older illustrative source.
M. K.

Woman's jacket of velvet, hand-embroidered in coloured silks with a pattern of birds and butterflies.
Late 1870s–early 1880s
Given by Messrs Harrods Ltd
T.871-1913

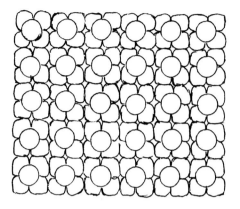

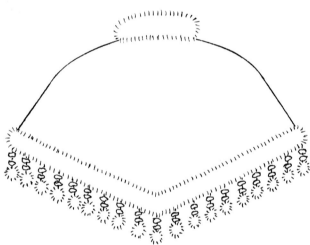

Russia's vast lands have provided resources not only of fashionable furs but also feathered specimens. This luxurious mantle of white down is a perfect example of the creative use of natural assets and reveals the ostentatious taste of the Russian elite. The mantle is almost weightless and its silky, sumptuous material is incredibly soft to the touch.

An ingenious but simple way of manipulating birds' down has been employed in its construction. It is made of cream silk entirely covered with links formed from stranded down shaped into roundels with cotton binding. The borders are trimmed with down, and the tufts have been hand-stitched to a cotton ground, to which are attached pendant down trimmings. The small roundels are reminiscent in shape of the much later flower trademark of Mary Quant. A narrow cream and yellow silk ribbon is stitched around the inside border, where a red manufacturer's stamp in Russian is still barely visible. The press studs down the front opening are most likely secondary additions.

A jacket similarly made and also dated to the 1860s survives in the Metropolitan Museum of Art in New York.
H. P.

Mantle of white down.
Russian, 1860s
Given by Miss H. M. Good
T.367-1982

This brown, high crowned, fur felt hat is elaborately trimmed, the brim with silk chenille and painted wooden beads, and the crown with silk ribbons and an extravagant decoration made from a mounted bird specimen and other contrived feather decoration. When the mode for wearing feathers, furs, stuffed birds and small mammals was at its height, the colours from even the most exotic species found in nature were not enough to meet the demands and whims of fashionable society.

Here, the head and neck section of a bird was treated with a colour wash to dye it to a rich bronze colour. This was augmented with several contrived sprays of feather plumes simulating spread wings and splayed out tail but made of feathers of a larger scale and type than that of the bird. These sprays, probably made from domestic fowl or other less costly species, have been similarly coloured to bronze then overpainted with an abstract design in shimmering golden bronze and green-gold paint of metallic lustre which would have caught the light in movement as if alive. Looking at the proportions of the head and long curved bill of the bird and a pale green iridescence showing through beneath the bronze colouring, it was most likely originally one of the more dull coloured but slightly iridescent females of a nectar-eating species, either a hummingbird or honeyeater. Hundreds of thousands of these species were sourced from South America and imported throughout Europe for the millinery trade.

M. K.

For more information on this outfit see page 26.

Woman's hat made of fur felt trimmed with silk chenille, painted wooden beads, silk ribbons and bird.
'Modes du Louvre'. French, about 1884
T.715-1997

 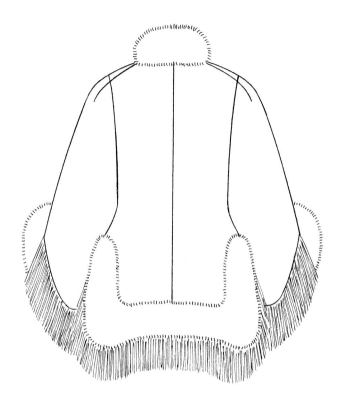

This exquisite dolman-sleeved jacket of the 1880s was the epitome of luxury and good taste. It was also highly fashionable in combining fur as a trimming and a feather design in the fabric, elements from the natural world which fascinated society at the time.

Made in the fashion house of Emile Pingat from expensive materials, it was a garment that only a wealthy, well-to-do society lady could afford. Although open only from 1860–96, the Paris fashion house of Pingat was as highly esteemed as that of Charles Worth and known for superb craftsmanship and elegance.

The sumptuous fabric is a silk voided velvet incorporating a design of ostrich feathers as the textured motif and focus of the pattern. The neck and fronts, cuffs and hems are edged with wide bands of white arctic fox (*Canis lagopus*) and deep fringes of silk chenille trimming. Arctic fox was an expensive and luxurious fur which would have been trapped in the wild, most likely in northern Canada, and imported through London.

The dolman is lined with cream machine-quilted satin so would have been warm to wear. It has a single hooked fastening at the neck and was designed to fall straight down and have a smooth line at the front, and for the back to sit neatly over the fashionably exaggerated bustle of the time.

M. K.

Dolman of silk voided velvet. Trimmed with white fox and chenille silk fringe.
Emile Pingat, Paris. French, about 1885
Given by Mrs G. T. Morton
T.64-1976

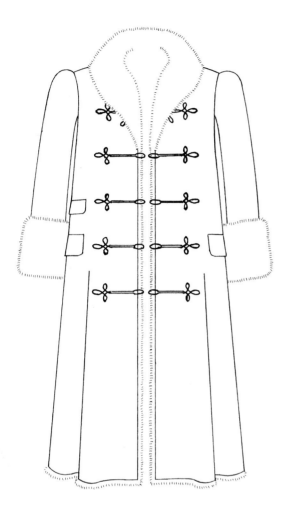 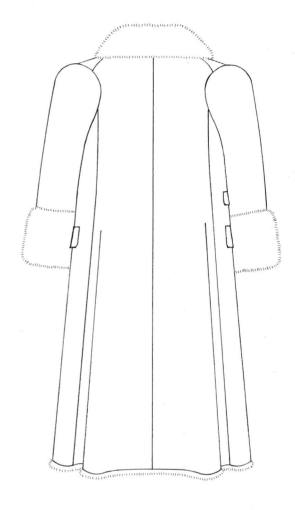

Until the mid-nineteenth century the primary use of furs in fashionable dress was as linings and accessories and for trimming ladies' gowns. Furs were worn by both men and women and were an indispensable item of luxury and a way of displaying wealth for the newly prosperous classes. A huge variety of furs were in demand by fashionable society which were imported from all over the world. The fur sales held in London were of primary importance to the international fur trade, with many furs being supplied from Canada and northern Europe, but tens of thousands of skins were also sold through the annual Russian fur sales and fairs held at Irbit, Nijini Novgrod and Moscow.

This overcoat is fully lined with wolf-skin except for the sleeves and has a deep collar and cuffs of wolf-skin. It is fastened with olivets and is trimmed with five rows of frogging made from a heavy black braid, one set being placed high on the chest so, when fastened, the fur collar could be turned up at the back and pulled up around the face at the front. The coat has two large pockets with flaps and there is a ticket pocket on the proper right side.

The skins of thirty-two wolves were used to make the lining and trimmings for this coat. All would have been trapped from the wild as fur farming was not established at the time. The pelts are of natural colour and undyed. Each pelt was trimmed to a rectangular shape, being used as large as possible, and joined skin on skin (rump to head) to make the lining. The skins are not perfectly matched and there are colour and quality discrepancies between them, but as they were used for lining purposes the visual effect of having all the skins alike must have been regarded as of little importance. Exact matching of the skins until thirty-two were found exactly alike would also have been excessively and unnecessarily costly for a lining.

M. K.

Man's overcoat of black wool lined with Russian wolf (*Canis lupus*).
Probably British, 1850s–90s
Given by Mrs A. Pollock
T.55-1951

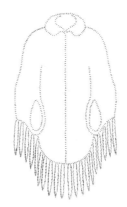

This mink tail trimming is from a mid-1880s lady's jacket of natural mid-brown mink (*Mustela vison*) (see line drawings). The jacket is hip length with curved arms and dolman sleeves. It has a small collar which closes at the neck and long pendant ends at the front. The back is shaped to accommodate and sit over a bustle and the entire hem is trimmed with mink tails. The jacket is lined with quilted brown satin.

Until the middle of the nineteenth century it was unusual to have a fur garment made up with the fur on the outside, and this jacket is one of the earliest mink jackets in any collection and can be precisely dated because of its particular style and cut.

Mink was an expensive and luxury fur, although over 300,000 skins were imported and sold through the London fur auctions annually at this date. The skins came via North American or Canadian fur trappers and were retailed by the Hudson Bay Furriers in London. The mink pelts are of excellent quality and well matched, which further indicates that this was an expensive and high-quality garment. The first experiments in mink farming and captive breeding were not conducted until the late 1870s and selective breeding to obtain a strain which would breed true to type and colour was not undertaken until 1887. It is therefore reasonable to assume that all the pelts came from wild mink. The pelts are natural coloured and undyed and are joined together end on end. The convention of 'stranding' mink in its preparation by the furrier did not begin until a few years later at the end of the nineteenth or very early twentieth century.[1]

M. K.

1. 'Stranding' or 'dropping' a skin is a method by which a furrier cuts and sews together again each individual pelt in order to obtain a longer and more elegant shape of skin before joining them all together to make a garment.

Woman's dolman-sleeved jacket.
Hudson Bay Furriers, 110 Oxford Street, Manchester, and 50 Church Street, Blackpool. English, 1885
Given by Mrs A. C. Bryant
T.77-1975

In the nineteenth century ladies grew their hair long and wore it elaborately dressed in twisted braids, coiled plaits and curls according to the particular fashion of each decade. False hair pieces were often resorted to where nature had failed to provide, or when the chosen fashionable style needed a little extra help to achieve the desired look. The image and line drawing shows a false hair piece dating from the second half of the nineteenth century. This 'ringlet bunch' or 'set of side curls' is made from human hair and is closely sewn onto a braid foundation. The hairdresser or ladies' maid would have attached it to the ladies' coiffure using hairpins in much the same way as we would today.

Hair merchants imported most hair from Europe and sold it to the wigmakers for making all manner of hair additions. In the nineteenth century it was not regarded as appropriate or socially acceptable for a lady to cut her hair and wear it short or 'bobbed'. This fashion did not come in until the early 1920s. Occasionally a woman impoverished or in straightened circumstances would resort to selling her hair to earn a little money, but this was very much a last resort of a woman of good character.

M. K.

Ringlet bunch of human hair.
British, 1850s–80s
AP 24-1889

GLOSSARY

Basque An extension of the bodice below the waist.

Bertha A deep collar-like trimming encircling the top of a dress that has a low neckline.

Bias A term used for fabric cut on the cross, i.e. in a direction diagonal to the weave of the fabric.

Bolton thumb The thumb of the glove and its quirk (gusset) are cut in one piece to allow ample freedom of movement.

Bone channel Two layers of fabric are stitched together to form a channel into which a strip of whalebone, steel or cane is inserted.

Bouffant Nineteenth-century term denoting a puffed-out part of a dress.

Boxcloth A thick woollen cloth usually dyed a buff colour and often used for riding habits and overcoats.

Buffon A large diaphanous neckerchief of gauze swathed around the neck and shoulders and puffed out over the bosom. Fashionable in the 1780s and 1790s.

Burnouse A mantle or cloak with a hood.

Busk A length of metal, wood or whalebone inserted into the front of the corset to help mould the body to the desired silhouette. During the second half of the nineteenth century it was usually made of steel, divided into two parts with fastenings that connected them together.

Bustle A device for thrusting out the skirt at the back of the waist.

Casing A strip of fabric sewn into place vertically onto a dart or seam on the inside of a garment. A narrow length of material, usually whalebone, steel or cane, was then inserted into the slot formed by the casing and the end was closed securely with hand stitches. Casing can also hold a ribbon or tape for gathering.

Challis A lightweight, soft clothing fabric made from silk and worsted wool, first produced in Norwich in about 1832.

Chemisette A partially visible white muslin or lawn 'fill-in' worn under the bodice of a day dress which is cut low in front.

Cording A twisted cord made from hemp, cotton, linen, paper or Coraline (trade name given to the processed cane from the Mexican or Central American ixtle plant) is inserted into channels created by stitching two layers of fabric together. During the late nineteenth century, special sewing machines were developed to carry out string cording more efficiently.

Crinoline Fabric woven from horsehair and cotton or linen thread and used for stiffening petticoats or as a lining. By 1856 the term had also come to mean a structure composed of graduated hoops worn under skirts to distend them and preserve their shape. The most successful crinolines were made of spring steel and were also known as crinoline cages.

Dart A stitched fold of fabric used to help shape a garment.

Dolman A mantle characterized by loose, sling-like sleeves cut with the body of the garment so that it resembled half-jacket, half-cape.

Floss silk Untwisted silk fibres.

Flossing Decorative and functional stitches on a corset to keep the whalebone, steel or cane strips in place and to prevent them working their way out of the casings or channels.

Foreparts The fronts of a coat, jacket or waistcoat that cover the chest.

Fourchette Fork-shaped piece of leather forming the sides of the finger of a glove.

Gore (also known as gusset) Usually a triangular-shaped piece of fabric sewn into a garment to increase the width at one end and decrease it at the other.

Jacquard loom The jacquard loom was invented in 1801 by Joseph-Marie Charles Jacquard (1752–1834). Jacquard weaving came into general use in Britain during the 1830s and saved time and money as it allowed more complex patterns to be woven automatically than were possible by the labour-intensive techniques of the hand-operated drawloom.

Lambrequin Shaped panels of cloth, often used in a row hanging from a mantelpiece or pelmet, as decoration.

Lappets Long streamers, often of lace, hanging down on either side of the face and attached to an indoor cap. During the 1860s the term 'lappets' was also used for pendant fabric trimmings on waistbands.

Mantle A cloak-like outer garment. From the 1870s onwards, also used to describe a dolman (see above).

Needleweaving A technique often used in passementerie whereby threads, often in contrasting colours, are passed in and out of threads laid down vertically by a needle rather than a shuttle.

Notch An indentation or incision on an edge or surface. In nineteenth-century tailoring the term was used to describe the gap cut between the collar of a coat/waistcoat and the lapel.

Olivet An oval button or mould covered in threads and used for fastening a garment by means of a loop or braid.

Padding stitches (also known as padstitching) Small stitches used in tailoring to sew layers together to shape and/or add body to a garment section.

Passementerie A French term covering a wide range of trimmings used to decorate, accentuate and complement elements of the furnished interior or dress. It is a generic term and includes tassels, braid, cord, gimp, tufts, rosettes and fringing.

Patch pocket A pocket applied to the outside of a garment, often used on sportswear, tailored dresses and informal wear. It is made from a separate pocket shape, usually cut from material that matches the pattern and grain of the fabric section it will cover.

Pelisse A woman's front-fastening, ankle-length garment usually made with sleeves. It was designed to be worn outdoors, rather like a coat, and followed the fashionable line of the dress underneath.

Peplum A short, gathered, pleated and/or trimmed piece of fabric attached at the waist of a woman's dress or jacket to create a decorative or drapery effect.

Piping with cord A thin cord covered in fabric and used to decorate clothing or soft furnishings and to reinforce seams.

Pique or lapped seam In glovemaking, where one edge of the leather overlaps the other so that one raw edge can be seen on the outside of the leather.

Plush A woven fabric with a very long pile.

Points In glovemaking, the lines of stitching which give subtle shaping to the back of a glove.

Polonaise The draped skirt of a robe or gown which revealed a petticoat or underskirt. The style was fashionable in the 1770s and again in the 1860s and 1870s.

Prix seam In glovemaking, where the cut edges are placed together and stitched on the outside with a running stitch so that both raw edges show.

Quirk Small diamond- or triangular-shaped piece of leather used as a gusset between the fingers or at the base of the thumb of a glove.

Revers (also known as a lapel) The turned-back edge of a coat, waistcoat or bodice.

Rouleau A narrow tube of bias-cut fabric, seamed and turned inside out so that the raw edges are inside. In the nineteenth century wadding was inserted into the tube to give it a firm shape. Rouleaux were used as dress trimmings, especially to add weight and/or decorative effect to the bottom of a skirt.

Russia braid A narrow braid with a herringbone weave, suitable for ornamenting military tunics and jackets and also used as a trimming on men's and women's fashionable dress.

Shirring Several rows of gathers used for a decorative finish.

Skirt The part of a coat or dress that hangs below the waistline.

Slipper A light slip-on shoe, especially one used for dancing.

Slot-and-stud fastening A metal fastening used on the front of corsets whereby a stud on one side of the split-busk slotted into a keyhole-shaped plate on the other.

Spangle (also known as sequin) A small, thin disc of metal, typically sewn onto clothing as decoration.

Spencer A short, close-fitting jacket worn by women and children in the early nineteenth century.

Stand collar An upright collar of a coat or waistcoat, constructed without a turn-down.

Stomacher A decorative V-shaped panel worn by women in the late seventeenth century and much of the eighteenth century to fill in the front of the bodice between the edges of an open-fronted gown.

Superfine A superior quality of broadcloth often used to make men's fashionable nineteenth-century coats.

Swelled edge A distinctive line of stitching positioned back from the edges (foreparts, pockets, vents, etc.) of a man's or woman's tailored garment.

Turn-down collar A collar constructed with a 'fall' (upper part) which turns down over the 'stand' (neck-band).

Vandyked edge A trimming with an edge shaped into large points. The name is taken from details on seventeenth-century portraits by Sir Anthony Van Dyck.

Velveteen A cotton fabric with a pile resembling velvet.

Vent An opening or slit in a garment.

Voided velvet Velvet is a pile weave in which the pile warp is raised in loops above the ground weave. These loops may be cut at a later stage. Voided velvet is an area of the fabric where no pile has been woven in.

Waist-tape (also known as a belt-tape) A band attached to the lining at the centre back of many late nineteenth-century women's bodices and outdoor garments. It fastened at the front with hooks and eyes and helped anchor the bodice and give a closer fit.

Whalebone (also known as baleen) Although the term 'whalebone' is commonly used, baleen is not bone. It is a keratin material (fibrous protein) more closely allied to horn. It is found in the mouths of whales and some other marine mammals, where it is formed into elongated triangular plates which are used as food strainers.

FURTHER READING

Arnold, Janet, *Patterns of Fashion: Englishwomen's Dresses and Their Construction 1660–1860* (London, 1977)

Arnold, Janet, *Patterns of Fashion: Englishwomen's Dresses and Their Construction c.1860–1940* (London, 1977)

Bradfield, Nancy, *Costume in Detail, 1730–1930* (Kent, 2003)

Breward, Christopher, *The Hidden Consumer: Masculinities, Fashion and City Life 1860–1914* (Manchester, 1999)

Browne, Clare, *Lace from the Victoria and Albert Museum* (London, 2004)

Burman, Barbara (ed.), *The Culture of Sewing* (Oxford, 1999)

Byrde, Penelope, *Nineteenth-Century Fashion* (London, 1992)

Carr, Raymond, *English Fox-Hunting: A History* (London, 1976)

Chenoune, Farid, *A History of Men's Fashion* (Paris, 1993)

Coleman, Elizabeth Ann, *The Opulent Era: Fashions of Worth, Doucet and Pingat* (London, 1989)

Cumming, Valerie, *Gloves: The Costume Accessories Series* (London, 1982)

Cunnington, C. Willett and Phillis, *Handbook of English Costume in the Nineteenth Century* (London, 1959)

Cunnington, C. Willett, *English Women's Costume in the Nineteenth Century* (New York, 1990)

Cunnington, C. Willett and Phillis, *A Dictionary of English Costume, 900–1900* (London, 1960)

Cunnington, C. Willett and Phillis, *The History of Underclothes* (New York, 1992)

Garfield, Simon, *Mauve: How One Man Invented a Colour that Changed the World* (London, 2000)

Gordon, S.S., *Turn-of-the-Century Fashion Patterns and Tailoring Techniques* (New York, 2000)

Harris, Kristina (ed.), *Authentic Victorian Dressmaking Techniques* (New York, 1999)

Hefford, Wendy, *Design for Printed Textiles in England from 1750–1850* (London, 1999)

Holding, T.H., *Late Victorian Women's Tailoring: The Direct System of Ladies' Cutting (1897)* (1997)

Howarth, Stephen, *Henry Poole, Founders of Savile Row: The Making of a Legend* (Honiton, 2003)

Irwin, John, *The Kashmir Shawl* (London, 1973)

Levitt, S., *Victorians Unbuttoned: Registered Designs for Clothing, their Makers and Wearers, 1839–1900* (London, 1986)

Montgomery, Florence M., *Textiles in America 1650–1870* (New York)

Newton, Stella Mary, *Health, Art & Reason: Dress Reformers of the Nineteenth Century* (London, 1974)

Parry, Linda, *British Textiles from 1850 to 1900* (London, 1993)

Pratt, Lucy and Woolley, Linda, *Shoes* (London, 1999)

Ribeiro, Aileen, *Ingres in Fashion* (New Haven & London, 1999)

Rothstein, Natalie, *Woven Textile Design in Britain from 1750–1850* (London, 1994)

Steele, Valerie, *The Corset: A Cultural History* (New Haven & London, 2001)

Steele, Valerie (ed.), *Encyclopedia of Clothing and Fashion* (3 volumes) (New York, 2005)

Taylor, Lou, *Mourning Dress: a Costume and Social History* (London, 1983)

Walkley, Christina and Foster, Vanda, *Crinolines and Crimping Irons. Victorian Clothes: How They Were Cleaned and Cared For* (London, 1978)

Warren, Philip, *Foundations of Fashion, The Symington Corsetry Collection 1860–1990* (Leicestershire, 2001)

Waugh, Norah, *The Cut of Men's Clothes 1600–1900* (London, 1987)

Waugh, Norah, *The Cut of Women's Clothes 1600–1900* (London, 1987)

Waugh, Norah, *Corsets and Crinolines* (New York, 1996)

Zakin, Michael, *Ready-Made Democracy: A History of Men's Dress in the American Republic, 1760–1860* (Chicago, 2003)

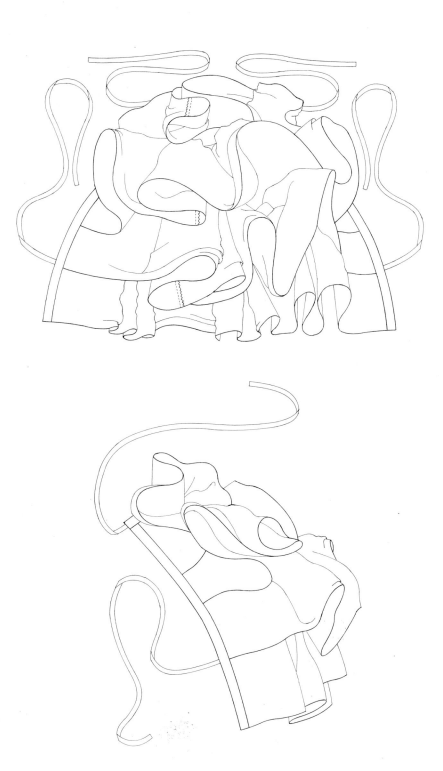

This detail, taken from a bustle of 1870–75, shows the stiff layered folds of horsehair and linen fabric. This fabric was known as 'crinoline', derived from 'crin', the French term for horsehair.[1]

The bustle is constructed using three curved horizontal steels held by a vertical steel applied to a fabric ground. This base supports the four gathered rows of horsehair and linen fabric which can be seen above. The shape is obtained by two lacing bands, each fitted with three eyelet holes, which when pulled up and laced cause the back of the bustle to curve and be held firmly in shape. There are hooks at the waist allowing the bustle to fasten onto a petticoat and two pairs of ties to secure the bustle around the waist and hips.

M. K.

1. The fabric was also used to make stiff petticoats used to distend and hold in shape the large skirts of the 1840s. The term crinoline was later used for the graduated spring-steel hoops used for the larger skirts of the 1850s and 1860s.

Bustle made of horsehair woven with linen.
British, 1870–75
Given by Miss Barbara V. Cooper
T.168-1937

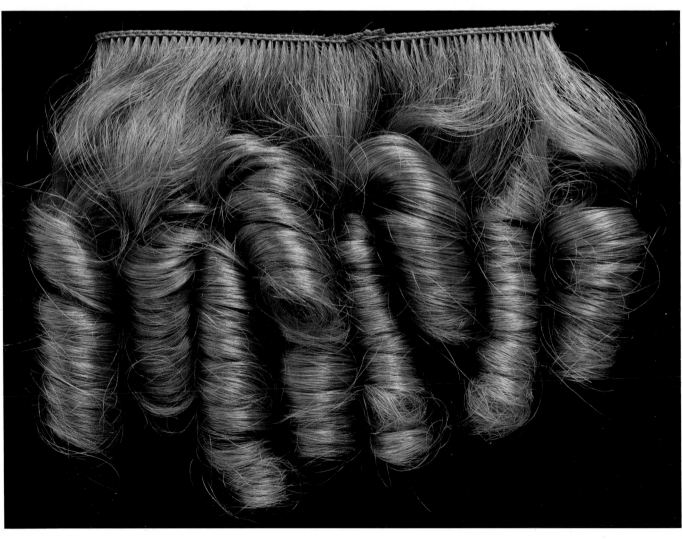